MW00398627

CHRONOPHONE Gaumont

"Gaumont"

PRÉSENTE DANS LES MEILLEURS CINÉMAS
LE GRAND FILM DOCUMENTAIRE

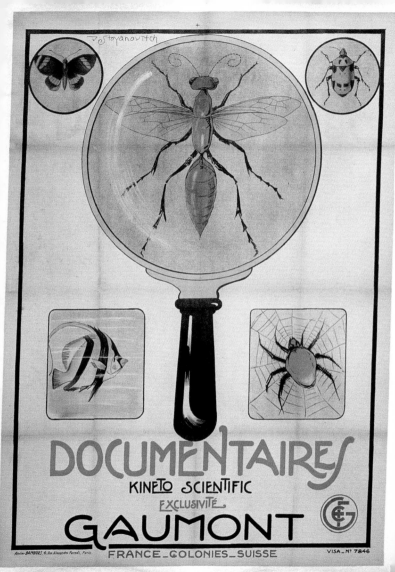

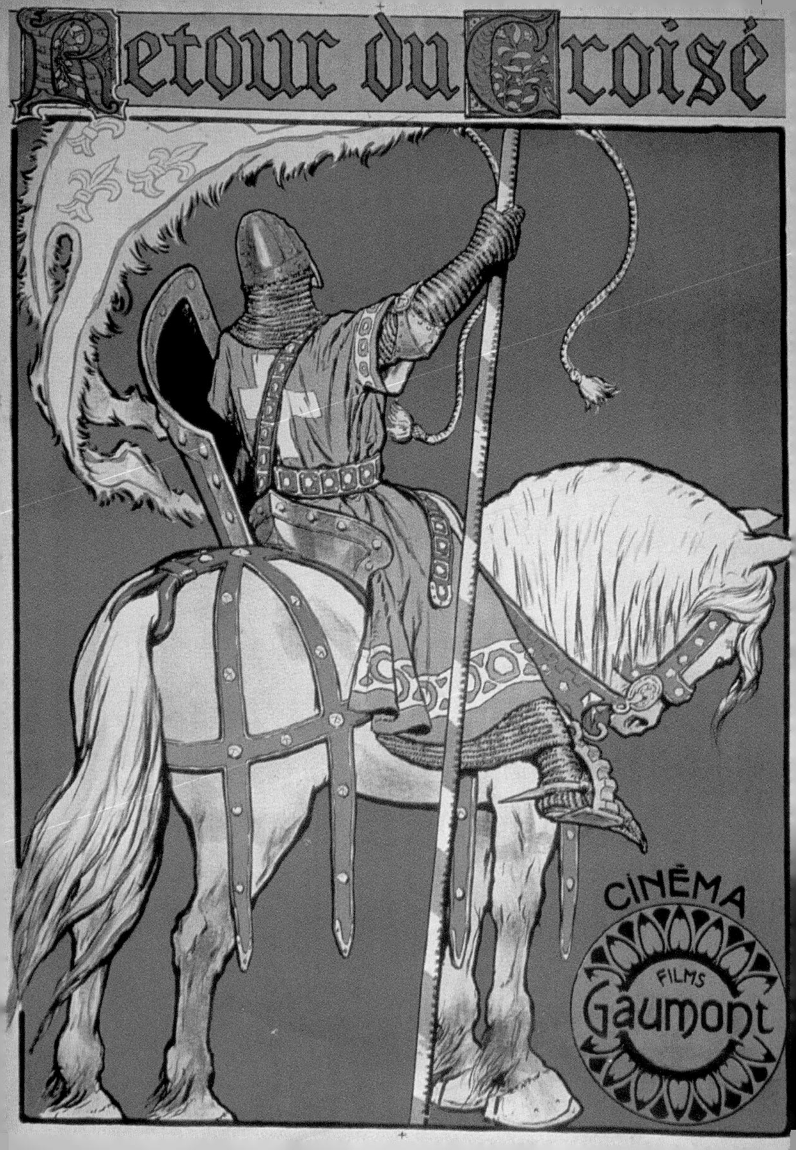

Retour du Croisé
CINÉMA
FILMS
Gaumont

SCARAMOUCHE

de **REX INGRAM**

La plus grande production cinématographique de l'année

Metro

Superproduction **LOEW METRO**

Gaumont distributeur

LE STIGMATE

Grand roman-ciné en 6 chapitres de Louis **FEUILLADE** & Maurice **CHAMPREUX**
adapté en roman par Paul **CARTOUX**

COMPTOIR
CINÉ
LOCATION
GAUMONT
35
Rue du Plateau
PARIS

PUBLIÉ PAR
Le Petit Journal

FILM
Gaumont

2ᵉ CHAPITRE : **LES DEUX MÈRES**

GAUMONT-FRANCO-FILM-AUBERT présente
BOUBOULE 1er ROI NÈGRE
G. MILTON
GRAPHILUX Tél 14.06.16 Bruxelles

François Garçon is the head of a French film completion guarantor, Films Garantie Finance. Garçon, who has a Ph.D. in history, has written and directed historical films. He has also written several books on the relationships between cinema and history, including *De Blum à Pétain, Cinéma et Société Française, 1936-1944,* (Le Cerf, 1984). Garçon is a coauthor of *Le Televisioni in Europa* (Foundation Giovanni Agnelli, Turin, 1990) and *Cinéma et Histoire, autour de Marc Ferro* (Cinémaction, 1992).

ISBN 0-8109-2579-6 Printed in Evreux, France, by Kapp Lahure Jombart.

Translated from the French by Bruce Alderman and Jonathan Dickinson.

To celebrate the Gaumont centennial, the French Ministry of Foreign Affairs is planning retrospectives in several countries of a number of films produced by Gaumont.

GAUMONT
A CENTURY OF FRENCH CINEMA

François Garçon

HARRY N. ABRAMS, INC.
PUBLISHERS

Paris—August 5, 1880. Place: the courtyard of the Collège Sainte Barbe. The principal announced: "First prize in mathematics. First prize in physics and natural science. First prize in geography." The winner: "Léon Gaumont." The young boy's head spun. With scores like these, he was sure to get into a prestigious engineering school. But his victory was short-lived. Financial problems at home prematurely ended his studies. At sixteen, Léon had to look elsewhere.

CHAPTER ONE
BUILDING AN EMPIRE

Determined forehead, piercing and often stern gaze, Léon Gaumont (right: in his artillery uniform) built an empire big enough to rival the major American studios. In 1925 he founded Gaumont Metro Goldwyn (GMG) in association with Metro Goldwyn.

STÉRÉO BLOCK-NOTES

BLOCK-NOTES

...ES & CHEZ LES CONSTRUCTEURS, L. GAUMONT & C.ie PARIS

The company Léon Gaumont & Cie was created August 10, 1895 "to commercialize and manufacture photographic equipment", a domain in which it enjoyed a certain notoriety. Block-Notes—a "miniaturized" camera invented in 1900—was a big success among a rich clientele. With Stéréo Block-Notes, Gaumont introduced shooting in stereoscope (in relief). From the start the company also constructed equipment for "animated images". Léon Gaumont assigned Georges Demeny the task of conceiving a machine which combined the recording and projecting of those images.

Forced to quit school, Léon became an apprentice devoting all his spare time to his studies. He attended evening classes during the week and astronomy courses on Sunday mornings at the Trocadero Observatory. The Observatory's director took notice of Léon and appointed him to conduct some demonstrations. By year's end, he recommended Léon's zeal to the binocular manufacturer, Jules Carpentier, who hired him as a secretary in 1881. Léon's debut in the work force proved difficult, however. Blessed with a natural gift of inventiveness,

Léon soon clashed with the spirit of the time which called for conformity. Even Carpentier himself found it difficult to admit that a young man with no university degree could make valid technical suggestions. His time spent at the binocular manufacturer taught Léon Gaumont that it was better to have his own company in order to carry out his own projects.

A manufacturer rises from the ranks

First, Léon had to serve in the military. His exam results earned him the rank of major in the artillery. In the army he met other alumni from the Collège Sainte Barbe. He became close friends with Henri Maillard, whose sister he would marry in 1888. The young woman's dowry consisted, among other things, of a 200 square meter piece of land located on the rue des Alouettes in the Buttes Chaumont section of Paris—Gaumont's future home.

Once back in civilian life, Léon turned to Carpentier who introduced him to Max Richard, the owner of the Comptoir Général de la Photographie (the Photography Syndicate). Richard needed a manager and Léon was the ideal candidate: 28 years old, excellent connections, married, and father of two children. Also, Léon's knowledge of physics seemed limitless when compared to that of a businessman like Richard. Within a few months, he had established himself within the company and thanks to a subsequent lawsuit between Max and his brother, Léon Gaumont was able to buy out the firm. In 1895 he re-named it the Société Léon

In 1903 Léon Gaumont & Cie registered its logo at the Registrar's Office: a daisy with four letters written in its core, ELGE (pronounced "L" "G" for its founder's initials). The logo was stamped on all the equipment. As films didn't yet have opening credits, Léon ordered that the daisy be placed in one or two scenes in each film with the greatest care possible. For example in interior scenes "on plates which are to hang on walls next to other plates."

Presented by Léon Gaumont himself, (opposite) the Chronophotographe of Demeny using film 35 mm wide was ready in 1897. It was acclaimed by its clientele who were mostly arcade operators. The film, *Boulogne sur Mer*, a documentary whose director is unknown, is listed as entry 1 in the Gaumont library. It was a triumph.

Gaumont & Compagnie. The brand name—Gaumont —was born. In the beginning, the new company only manufactured and sold optics and photographic equipment.

A major event drastically changed the future direction of Gaumont & Cie. In 1895, the Lumière brothers introduced their Cinématographe. Gaumont immediately knew what this meant: moving pictures could bring in a fortune. So he decided to devote all his efforts to making movie projectors. In the summer of 1896, the rue des Alouettes factory brought out the Chrono "Demeny", the first Gaumont projector.

Manufacturing was one thing, but commercializing the product was quite another. Indeed with so many competitive models on the market, Gaumont had to find a way to make his projectors stand out from the crowd and appeal to potential clients who were essentially carnival show operators. Already, Lumière, with his picture, *L'Arroseur Arrosé*, had shown the way: projectors had to have something to project. So in early 1897, Gaumont founded a film production department. By April, the first film library was created.

From manufacturing to film production...

For Gaumont, as for most other companies at the time, making pictures was just a by-product of

In order to satisfy the customer who was starting to get bored by the silent images, sound was added—often a piano accompaniment which would cover-up the sounds of the projector and underscore the action in the film. Sometimes the services of a sound effects team were used. Experimental talking films using the Chronophone developed by Gaumont (left) helped pick up admissions which were sagging at the time. All Gaumont equipment was manufactured in workshops on the rue des Alouettes (right).

In its early days, the moving picture industry saw some strange characters: dwarves, magicians, fire-eaters and an audience who—on Sundays—would get their entertainment by answering the calls of carnival barkers. The films—projected in uncomfortable shacks — were often only part of the show. The cinema had a hard time finding itself a name. It was alternately called "Théâtre Aérogyne", "Gioscope", or even "Lentielectroplasticroni-mocoliserpentographe".

making equipment. Thus, the real business and financial stakes were in the manufacturing of this equipment for the arcade shows and, after 1905, for the first motion picture theaters. The required investment was considerable but Gaumont was holding some strong cards. From the start, he teamed up with influential bankers—such as the Banque

"In Belleville, next to the workshops [...], they gave me an unused terrace with cement floors (which made it impossible to fix real sets); it had a shaking glass-covered roof and opened-up onto a waste land. [As a backdrop] : a sheet painted by a painter of hand-held fans from the neighborhood, as a set, a row of wooden cabbages cut-out by the carpenters, costumes rented here and there [...] As actors: my comrades, a crying baby and his worried mother who jumped up every time right into the camera's field of vision [...]. That's how *La Fée aux Choux* ["The cabbage fairy"] was born.**"**

Alice Guy,
Autobiographie d'une pionnière du cinéma

Suisse et Française—and with businessmen such as Gustave Eiffel and Joseph Vallot, the director of the Mount Blanc observatory. Gaumont, a scientist with the temperament of an industrialist, encouraged and often personally guided technical innovations. He was also able to measure costs. From 1897, he filed one patent after another. At the time, the company had only 12 staffers and nearly all its resources went into the technical side of the business.

Production or "cinematographic publishing", as it was called, remained only a minor preoccupation. Nevertheless Léon didn't say "no" when in 1897, his 24-year old secretary, Alice Guy, offered to make films based on scripts. (The only condition was that it should not encroach on her job as a secretary.) In so doing Alice Guy became the world's first woman movie director. Her talent was acclaimed in films hardly two minutes long, such as *Déménagement à la Cloche de Bois*, *Sur les Barricades*, *L'Ivresse* and *Volée par les Bohémiens*.

The Paris World Fair of 1900 confirmed the public's fascination with moving pictures. Yet, the same year, the Lumière brothers decided to cease producing films. For Gaumont, this was a godsend. The company immediately increased moving picture production but not at the expense of its technical efforts. In fact, camera magazines had to be adapted to the new, lengthier films; electrical motors had to be designed for the new projectors; and laboratories had to be built to develop the massive amounts of footage that were being shot. Five years later, in 1905 at the Buttes Chaumont, Léon Gaumont opened the Théâtre

"Mademoiselle Alice" (below left), like Méliès, believed that scenes should be acted out in front of a camera instead of just filming real life which was how Gaumont, Lumière and Pathé had been making films. From 1897 until she left France for the States in 1907, she made more than 370 movies (left, from top to bottom: *La Fée aux Choux*, *L'Electrocutée*, *Le Testament de Pierrot*). Inset: Alice Guy directing a Phonoscène or talking film, *Mignon*, by the composer Ambroise Thomas. The picture shows the first phase of talking pictures. The sound was first recorded on a wax disk and then the images were filmed. Synchronization was achieved by having the actors lipsinc the scene during filming.

Cinématographique Gaumont—a 45 meter long by 43 meter high studio. The floor was designed, according to the brochure, "to stand the weight of a herd of elephants".

...and on to distribution

Thanks to all these activities the company acquired real financial clout. In 1906, the Société des Etablissements Gaumont—SEG—was created with a capital of 2.5 million francs. Pierre Azaria, head of the Compagnie Générale d'Electricité, was named president. At the same time, the Banque Suisse et Française (the future Crédit Commercial de France,

From the very beginning, Gaumont experimented in color using the Trichrome process: a lens divided into three primary colors—blue, red and yellow. Above: the beach at Deauville for a documentary filmed in 1913 using Trichrome.

In December 1906 Gaumont & Cie became SEG, Société des Etablissements Gaumont, with a capital of 2 million French Francs. The capital increased to 3 million and finally 4 million by 1913. On the eve of World War I, SEG shareholders included Banque de Bâle, Banque Suisse et Française, Banque Robert and Gustave Eiffel. Below: Edgar Costil, the head of Gaumont distribution, and his staff.

and Gaumont's long-standing partner) strengthened its position within the company.

As Léon gathered awards, the company continued to grow and evolve with the changing times of the industry. Until 1908 films were sold outright. Buyers were able to show them as many times as public demand warranted. But this all changed when Gaumont's competitor, Charles Pathé, claimed that a movie is "a literary and artistic property" subject to copyright. Pathé stopped selling his films in February. He then set up five companies and gave them the sole right to commercialize Pathé films. From then on Pathé's moving pictures would be rented to "member" clients for a limited number of showings. Modern film distribution was born.

Throughout the country movie theaters sprang up as community halls were converted into film houses with the aid of local governments. As a result the market expanded its demographic reach as shopkeepers and office workers became moviegoers.

Fall 1911, Paris high society crowded the place Clichy for the inauguration of the world's largest movie theater (3,400 seats), the Gaumont Palace. The conversion of the former racetrack which was constructed for the 1900 World Fair lasted several months. The interior decoration was sky blue in step with the Pompeii style popular at the time. The usherettes—who were really attendants — were dressed in sky blue uniforms and caps. Posh beyond any contemporary equal, the Palace attracted a high-class audience who were welcomed by a certain Beanzin, the doorman who according to legend was the son of the king of Dahomey. In the back of the theater, small tables with lamp-shaded lights permitted customers to eat and drink while watching the film, a common practice in café-concert halls.

GAUMONT · PALACE

DIRECTION : GAUMONT · LOEW · METRO

PROGRAMME OFFICIEL GRATUIT

Photo de marcel arthaud

Le Browning
Grand Film Artistique "GAUMONT" - Dramatique

LE THÉATRE AUTOMATIQUE
"Le Commissaire est Bon Enfant"
Scène en 1 acte, tirée de la célèbre Pièce de Courteline

BOUT DE ZAN vole un Éléphant
Comique

ENTR'ACTE

TROISIÈME PARTIE

stre. Mazurka Hongroise . . . . G. BERNARD

Les 4 DELTONS
Strong-Acrobates & Equilibristes

Les Echinodermes
Scientifique

A LUMIÈRE & L'AMOUR
Grand Cinémadrame "Gaumont"

ristes Aventures d'ONÉSIME
Comique

umont-Palace-Actualités

Gaumont-Palace, Retraite... Paul FOSSE.

réserve toute modification au présent Programme

DU 9 AU 15 MAI

ntation du Grand Film d'Aventures

"FANTOMAS"
Tiré du célèbre Roman de MM. SOUVESTRE & ALLAIN

BOUT DE ZAN
VOLE UN ÉLÉPHANT

The Gaumont Palace offered an entire evening of entertainment for the whole family. An orchestra performed opening and closing numbers. Live acts and frequent intermissions were programmed in between the handful of films screened daily including documentaries, short subjects, newsreels and the featured film.

Triste Aventure d'ONÉSIME

The theater was often sold out in advance thanks to the loyal following of stars *Bout de Zan* and *Onésime*. Prices ranged from 50 centimes for the gallery to 18 Francs for an orchestra loge. The program was family-oriented with a high moralistic tone. Below: Renée Carl who played the mother in the Bébé Abelard series 1910-13. Below, left : an ad for "Ben Hur perfume" published in a program for the Gaumont Palace during the film's run.

Le parfum...
BEN·HUR
BROCARD
PARIS

In 1910 Gaumont adopted this new system of distribution and founded the Comptoir Ciné-Location, naming Edgar Costil—who came from the music publishing business—as director. The new company also handled equipment sales and theater operations—Gaumont now owned movie theaters. Indeed, Léon Gaumont understood that theaters had the double advantage of collecting receipts directly at the box office and of being the showcase for the company's technical innovations. As for the boss himself, he was still actively involved on all fronts. That same year, for example, he presented the Chronophone before the Academy of Sciences. And

Not all of the shoots took place at the Buttes Chaumont studios. When the action called for it, the film crew moved into some surprising locations. Here on the roof of the Gaumont Palace for *Onésime Débute au Théâtre* directed by Jean Durand.

Former wine merchant turned journalist, Louis Feuillade (below) began his film career by writing scripts for Gaumont. He was first hired by Alice Guy as an assistant. Upon her departure he became "head of theater services and filming", meaning he was responsible for choosing scripts, actors and directors. He held that post until his death in 1925. He also directed 642 films, first making ten-minute shorts and then serials.

two years later at the Olympia, he pleaded the case for talking pictures—way ahead of his time. On July 15, 1910, Gaumont purchased the Place de Clichy Racetrack and unveiled its ambitious designs: soon the Gaumont trademark—the daisy—was to fly over the world's largest movie theater: the Gaumont Palace.

A Gaumont style

Although he was technically minded, Léon didn't completely ignore the artistic aspect of film producing. Every Tuesday, he and his assistants would review the film output. Léon would interject comments which were as expeditious as they were lethal: "You can pick up your check and leave!" or "You should take up another trade!" During these sessions, Léon proved that he had a good nose for popular taste. After attending the showing of Pathé comedy films in New York, he wrote to Louis Feuillade, who had succeeded Alice Guy in 1907 : "We too must have good scripts. Instructions for the actors can often save a film."

Léon and Feuillade agreed on one point: they both obstinately refused to waste anything. Until 1914, Gaumont productions were always shot in the most economical conditions possible.

While American directors borrowed heavily from French comic films, French film-makers adopted an American genre which would soon become a major force — the western. In 1911 Jean Durand directed for Gaumont "Scènes de la vie de l'Ouest américain" (Scenes From the Life of the American West): *Cent Dollars Mort ou Vif, Pendaison à Jefferson City, Le Railway de la Mort*, etc.—shot in the Camargue in Southern France. Legend had it that Joe Hamman (left, facing off with Gaston Modot) was a cowboy in the US. He specialized in this genre.

Cinema began with news footage: the arrival of a train. But it would not be until 1910 before Gaumont launched *Gaumont Actualités*—a weekly newsreel. Highly popular, newsreels were eventually integrated into the movie house program.

Léon had once stated: "I have no intention of allowing my movie directors to spend without taking cost into account." Examples: when locations were used and the action took place in squalid neighborhoods, they would then shoot in the vicinity of the company headquarters at the Elgé complex at Buttes Chaumont.

If the action required a lot of extras, Gaumont employees were called in from the workshops. Towards 1911, when Feuillade began making longer films and shooting had to be done in the studio, Gaumont stopped building realistic and expensive sets. Instead they used simple, painted backdrops. The company would quickly make adaptations of popular American films. *Bronco Bill*, a big hit overseas, became *Arizona Bill* in its French version.

The result of all this helped create a Gaumont style which was distinguishable on the screen. Instead of costly action or chase sequences, Gaumont films were characterized by psychological dramas or vaudeville comedies which the puritanical Léon had purged of any tawdry suggestiveness.

Starting as early as 1905, the company began putting actors and directors under contract. This policy was aimed at creating a stable of talent.

In the early days of cinema, kids were king. The stars were named Bébé (Baby), Bout de Zan, la petite Susy (Little Susy). These children-stars were naturally great actors. The only real problems came from the parents who sometimes got too greedy demanding exceedingly high payments for their offspring. This was the reason why Feuillade replaced Bébé—who was hired when five years old—by the boy who co-starred as his little brother in *Bébé Adopte un Petit Frère* (opposite): René Poyen, renamed Bout de Zan, four years old. A rascal, terrorizer of nannies and mothers, he was the joy of moviegoers aged 7 to 77.

Each director chose his own crew and cast. Jean Durand filmed with the Pouites, music hall and circus acrobats. Among whom was his wife, Berthe Dagmar (below).

Besting its competitors, Gaumont offered multi-film contracts to actors. For example, Musidora Renée Carl and Bébé, as well as Bout de Zan signed year-long contracts.

In 1910 the Newsreel Service—*Gaumont Actualités*—was launched. The week's topics were presented to Léon on Monday evenings. In the half-light of the projection room the boss tossed out his verdicts: "That parade is fine—give it 20 meters! The funeral is too long: cut to 10 meters!"

Feuillade and his serials

At the same time, Feuillade was organizing, creating and inventing. His low-budget serials combined non-stop action with uncomplicated characters. Other future greats also began their careers, including Emile Cohl whose *Fantasmagories* (1908) was the first cartoon in the world ; Léonce Perret, creator of the *Léonce* series; Jean Durand, author of the *Onésime* series; Henri Fescourt, and Bosetti, with his *Roméo* series, of which he was both director and star. Each became famous with the company and helped create a remarkable film library.

Fantômas (1913) reinforced Feuillade's popularity. Made-up of five episodes, the series ran six hours.

FANTÔMAS

Berthe Dagmar liked to act with strange partners: elephants, tigers or snakes.

Production grew constantly. New studios were built on the high plains of Cimiez, near Nice — only a day's train ride from Paris. The company was taking advantage of the mild Mediterranean climate to cut its electricity costs.

In 1912 film credits mentioned actors' names for the first time and in the following year, riding a wave of success, Feuillade launched the famous *Fantômas*—the first Gaumont serial. No longer forced to shoot in the studios, Feuillade took actors on the weirdest locations.

The Gaumont Empire

By the spring of 1914, the Elgé complex had become a major film corporation and a sprawling enterprise. Alongside the projector assembly lines were film developing laboratories, workshops for mechanics, painters, decorators, carpenters and costume designers, studios, and storerooms for stage sets. Upstairs, along with the crowded rooms for the

America lands. Here, in 1917, American newsreel reporters prepare to leave for the front.

reading committees, were the departments where all of the company's advertising campaigns and posters were conceived and fabricated. To enable the production to flow smoothly, a world-wide network was operating night and day. A huge map showed the locations of offices and shooting studios in New York, Montreal, London, Berlin, Vienna, Moscow, Budapest, Calcutta, Saigon, Barcelona, Casablanca and Buenos Aires. The turnover mirrored the company's unbridled expansion: 900,000 francs in 1904, 25,000,000 francs in 1913.

World War I, a bitter victory

On August 6, 1914, the German army entered Belgium and shelled the city of Liège. But no one had yet fathomed what was to come. In early August, after a report on the Tour de France bicycle race, Gaumont newsreels showed footage of Kaiser Wilhelm playing tennis at the Baltic resort of Zoppot. It was only on August 19th that newsreels made their cautious entry into the war. The scarcity of battle pictures stemmed, in part, from the indecisiveness of the inexperienced military censors who did not quite know how to handle the newsreels.

Land around 12 rue des Alouettes was bought and adapted to the needs of Cité Elgé. The first film studio (the world's largest until 1914) was built in 1905 next to the photo development laboratories. A print shop for the fabrication of advertising material was founded in 1907. They were followed by film stock storage houses, studios and garages; workshops for designing posters and sets (left); and warehouses for furniture, wardrobes, costumes and other accessories. Nothing was missing, not even a menagerie. All of this in a factory setting complete with three large smoke stacks. Below: in 1924, Cité Elgé covered 24,000 square meters.

They hesitated between censorship—a complete ban of newsreels—and creating propaganda films (which seemed to be beyond their grasp). The Interior Minister's decree which created a film review board was not signed until June, 1916. The balance between propaganda and censorship was never struck.

In early October 1914, far from the front and in unfavorable conditions, movie theaters re-opened and production was resumed. The war effort was generously shared and the Société des Etablissements Gaumont did its part for the sake of the country. At the time, the company totalled 2,100 employees. Those who were drafted included carpenters,

painters, electricians, actors and directors. Gaumont first lost the services of Gaston Ravel, one of its foremost directors. Then, in March 1915, Louis Feuillade went off to war. In all, 200 Gaumont workers and technicians were either killed or wounded in combat.

Company profits were also sacrificed to the war effort. Projectionists were scarce in Lyon and technicians were rare in Paris where production was interrupted for lack of heat and electricity. Gaumont managers didn't know which way to turn. In the face of general shortage, orders came in for radio equipment for the aviation, projectors for the trenches, and goniometric instruments for the artillery.

During the first winter of the war, the company went into wartime production. Although the Army Film Section only began in February 1915, Gaumont dispatched its cameramen to the front line well

In 1917, mired down in the war, France could at least salute one hero, Feuillade's Judex. The serial kept the French on the edge of their seats. They had to wait until episode 12—episodes were written as they went along—before they could witness the death of villain Musidora.

before. Yet due to the belief that the footage could provide the enemy with information, they were never allowed on to the battlefield. This accounts for the abundance of film footage on the wounded and on new types of combat gear, and the lack of footage on the front line battles in the trenches.

Fiction, as well as news, made its contribution to the war effort. During the winter of 1914, Gaumont produced *Françaises Veillez*, *Le Héros de l'Yser* and *Mort au Champ d'Honneur*. And in 1915, in the same vein, *L'Empreinte de la Patrie*, *France et Angleterre for Ever*, *Les Poilus de la Revanche*, *Triple Entente*, and *L'Union Sacrée*.

Nevertheless, these patriotic films were not popular and made up no more than 5 % of the company's total output. By the spring of 1916, Gaumont decreased production of propaganda films. Only a few films of this type were listed for the year, including *L'Angélus de la Victoire* and *Marraines de France*. The twilight of patriotic glory was 1917 when only *The Deserter* was produced. The public was saturated with war and preferred the adventures of *Judex* to exaggerated tales of Gallic heroism. And

Gaumont's contribution to the war effort: an aerial camera mounted on the fuselage of the bomber Goliath permitted reconnaissance of enemy positions. Below, Léonce Perret's *Une Page de Gloire*—a patriotic movie.

finally, in 1918—before the allied victory had been assured—Gaumont produced *Les Enfants de France Pendant la Guerre*.

The sole winner: Hollywood

November, 1918. A victorious France became the top military force in Europe. The country was shattered but triumphant. Thanks to its Trichrome process, Gaumont released the victory parade in color. Yet

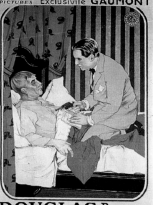

Léon's joy was short-lived for he realized that the war had cost his company the export market. America had successfully filled-in the world-wide void left open by the war-torn European movie industry. On top of that, the Russian and German markets closed-up due to post-war political and economic events. The situation was hardly

The Pax collection, launched in 1919, modernized film esthetics while maintaining its appeal for popular audiences. Léon Poirier, an adept of the theater, was artistic director of the collection. Under the Pax label, he produced *Narayana* (above left), *L'Ombre Déchirée*, and *Jocelyn* adapted from Lamartine. Marcel L'Herbier directed his first films under Poirier. At the same time, Feuillade continued his serials. (Center: *Le Fils du Flibustier*, 1922. Right: *L'Orpheline*, 1921.) Thanks to an exclusive distribution agreement with Paramount Pictures for a select number of titles, Gaumont introduced Mary Pickford, Douglas Fairbanks and John Gilbert to the French public.

better in Italy or in England, where the war had helped stimulate their national movie industries. Once peace had returned, their demand for French imports decreased dramatically. From this point on, revenues from exports would represent only a fraction of total sales. Now Gaumont had to rely solely on the French domestic market and therefore could no longer balance its books with revenues from foreign markets. In addition, production budgets rose, making it even harder to recoup the overall cost of a film. As a result, Gaumont slashed production: in 1914, it made 145 films. By 1919 this dropped to 11.

A difficult resurgence

Starting as early as 1913, Gaumont films had gotten longer. The day of the 90-minute standard feature film was fast approaching. Production was concentrated around a double axis: Louis Feuillade's serial films and the Pax collection.

Feuillade cranked out the serials. High volume meant lower costs and Léon Gaumont

Theater operators received information and material from the head office as well as suggestions on how to promote the films. Below: an ad for Feuillade's *Barrabas*.

welcomed the increase in productivity inspired by American production methods. Thanks to Louis Feuillade, Gaumont was able to fill its theatrical circuit's pipeline with serial films such as *Barrabas* (9 hours, 1919), *Les Deux Gamines* (8 hours, 1921), *L'Orpheline* (8 hours 30 minutes, 1921), *Le Fils du Flibustier* (7 hours 30 minutes, 1922).

The Pax collection—headed by Léon Poirier—was launched in 1919 and served as a reservoir of future talents. Many of France's great future directors would work with him : Jacques Feyder and Marcel L'Herbier directed Pax films. Other directors started as actors such as Claude Autant-Lara and René Clair. And finally famed actors such as Charles Boyer, Pierre Blanchar, Fernand Ledoux, Carette and Josette Day were cast either as anonymous extras or in some cases in lead parts.

The playful clowning of *Onésime* did not survive World War I while at the same time Charlie Chaplin became an international legend. In *Le Pied qui Etreint* (above) Jacques Feyder made a parody of the American comic.

For the role of Jean Vernier (opposite) in the series *Parisette* (1921), Louis Feuillade called upon a young man who had already appeared in *L'Orpheline*: René Clair. The future member of the Académie Française was taking his first steps in the cinema. After becoming a renowned director, Clair returned to Gaumont to direct *Les Belles de Nuit* in 1952 and *Les Fêtes Galantes* in 1966.

Despite this activity, the Société des Etablissements Gaumont was actually running out of steam. The markets were too small for its films. Gaumont was supplying only its own world-wide circuit. And this circuit had shrunk. Aside from Switzerland, Belgium and North Africa, the company could only rely on Egypt, Syria and Palestine. It went into the red, and all capital increases were used to pay off debt. From 4 million francs in 1913, the capital was increased to 5 million in 1919, then leaped to 10 million in 1921.

These capital increases meant Léon was destined to lose control of his company. (He resigned in 1932.) The Crédit Commercial de France—which had increased its shares in SEG—put its own men in

After the War Gaumont signed agreements with foreign companies, which included the Italians and the Swedish.

vous brûlez
d'envie de passer une bonne soirée, d'admirer un spectacle qui vous sorte des banalités courantes, vous iriez volontiers applaudir un beau film, mais lequel ?

L'ÉPREUVE DU FEU
l'œuvre magnifique de la **SVENSKA-FILM**, renferme toutes les qualités capables de satisfaire les plus difficiles : scénario émouvant et original, jeu pathétique d'artistes éminents, photographie splendide et mise en scène somptueuse.

Vous viendrez donc applaudir

L'ÉPREUVE DU FEU
ce beau film mis en scène par Victor SJOSTROM et interprété par Jenny HASSELQVIST, Gosta EKMAN, Ivan HEDQVIST & Tore SVENNBERG.

Gaumont   SVENSKA FILM

Rare image of the two great industrial rivals of the French cinema, Charles Pathé (on the right) and Léon Gaumont (on the left) posing for the same shot. Faced with harsh economic realities both men lost control of their companies after a series of capital increases.

place and was soon dictating strategy. To remedy its precarious financial situation, Gaumont began signing agreements with foreign firms. Distribution deals were inked with the Italian UCI and the Swedish firm, Svenska. French audiences owed their discovery of Mauritz Stiller and Victor Sjöström to Gaumont. American companies were not left out. In 1922, Films Loew Metro, SA, was created to run the Gaumont exhibition circuit. Three years later, the SEG teamed up with Metro Goldwyn for a distribution deal. King Vidor's *The Big Parade*, and Fred Niblo's *Ben Hur*, were distributed in France under the emblem of the Gaumont daisy.

Greta Garbo was not an unknown in Gaumont's movie theaters. In Fred Niblo's *The Temptress* (*La Tentatrice*, 1926) her co-star was Lionel Barrymore whose name does not appear on the poster.

Gaumont stops production

But these measures would no longer be enough. In 1925 Gaumont announced that, "until further order, it is no longer making films, except for the Louis Feuillade productions, which are being continued by his son-in-law". The decision was made after Léon Gaumont and Edgar Costil went to the United States and screened films to be distributed by Gaumont. Their trips confirmed the statistics: competing with the Americans was not simply one-sided—it was suicidal. Gaumont noticed that in California, sets were used once, then abandoned: "Do you think that could happen in France? Most certainly not!"

Then again, the United States had 25,000 theaters in need of new films each week. Those films would then go to Europe already amortized. How could the 4,500 French theaters compete with them when many were still mere converted itinerant theaters? The figures summed up the economic crisis: French production plummeted from 73 films in 1925 to 55 the following year, of which only three were by Gaumont. On the other hand, American movies were saturating the market with 444 imported in 1926. Worse yet, with their sense of show business and star-studded casts, those Hollywood productions turned out to be huge crowd-pleasers, and managed to take in no less than 80 % of the French box office receipts.

From now on the French had to deal with the major American studios. In 1925 the Société des Etablissements Gaumont signed with the powerful Metro Goldwyn to create a new company, Gaumont Metro Goldwyn (GMG), whose mandate was to distribute American films in France and French films in the United States. Thanks to GMG, a rich film library was offered to the French public. It included Buster Keaton and Lon Chaney as well as the great Hollywood extravaganzas. Below: *Ben Hur* played by Ramon Novarro ; the chariot race scene.

The world of cinema changed dramatically with the introduction of talking pictures. Gaumont placed all its bets on the new sound technology and radically transformed its studios and theaters. A move that was imperative but costly.

CHAPTER II
THE CRISIS YEARS

In 1929 the Société Nouvelle des Etablissements Gaumont introduced its universal sound projector, "Idéal Sonore"—Ideal Sound (right). Left: Dita Parlo, star of Jean Vigo's classic film, *L'Atalante*.

Filmed in Rumania in 1930, *Roumanie, Terre d'Amour* (left) was directed by Camille de Morlhon. On the posters Gaumont wanted it be known that the film had sound—not only music accompaniment but "talking and singing".

With film production on hiatus, Gaumont fought to maintain its market position in theatrical exhibition as well as in equipment manufacturing. Patents were filed regularly for new sound equipment inventions such as the Filmphone in 1927 and the Elgéphone in 1928. Léon Gaumont and his successors shared the conviction that sound on film and the amplification of sound in the theaters were the key to future success. Time was running out, however. Talking pictures were already conquering the marketplace. In 1929, the trades reported that of the 550 American films produced, two-thirds were talkies.

Sound, a costly extravagance

In theory Gaumont could win on two fronts: as sound equipment manufacturer and as theater circuit owner. But to do so it had to act fast. It needed more capital and more financial muscle. In 1929 it raised its capital to 24 million francs. Then in January 1930, Gaumont merged with Aubert Franco Film to create the Gaumont Franco Film Aubert (GFFA) and reached an agreement to buy Continsouza, whose projectors were used in numerous theaters. In order to fight against the tidal wave of foreign technology, Gaumont believed that bigger was better. Actually, France and Gaumont had already been outpaced in the sound equipment war. The technological battle

As a result of a merger which began in 1930, Louis Aubert (a future congressman) brought Gaumont a prestigious film library and 30 movie theaters, half of which were in Paris.

continued, however, as Gaumont put its hopes primarily in its Idéal Sonore projector.

Its own theaters had to be rapidly equipped. The public demanded more and more sophisticated sound technology: "Films with simple phonograph accompaniment disappoint a public which has already learned to appreciate the synchronized voice technique." In 1930, a theater would bring in 20,000 francs by showing a silent film. The same theater would bring in three times more with a synchronized film, and up to five times more with a talking film entirely in French. Regardless of the handsome rewards, modernization proved costly. For example, in May 1930 the Gaumont Palace closed

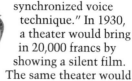

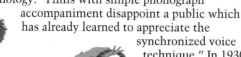

In its original version *Daïnah la Métisse* (left, 1931) counted 2,700 meters of film or one hour and ten minutes. Inspired by the expressionists and depicting an exotic tone which was judged perverse, the film by Jean Grémillon was highly disliked by Gaumont's top brass. They forced cuts which sliced the film down to 1,400 meters or 51 minutes. Grémillon refused to have his name associated with the chopped-up version.

for renovations "with the goal of creating an atmospheric cinema of 6,000 seats". Reconstruction lasted thirteen months during which Gaumont received no box office receipts. By year's end, France had 460 large theaters equipped with sound. Gaumont had outfitted 94 but Western Electric was the market leader with 106.

Paradoxically, credit was easy to obtain even during deep economic recession. The experts explained this by noting that "movies were France's most prosperous industry". In fact Paris box office receipts increased 33.5 percent from 1929 to 1930—an astounding feat considering that the annual rates since 1925 had been only between

La Tragédie de la Mine, *Kameradschaft* ("Comradship") in its original version, told the story, in a very realistic manner, of the catastrophe of Courrières in 1906 during which German miners came to the aid of their French comrades. The film was made in 1931 and its pacifist message was highly criticized by the nationalist press of the period. Director Georg Wilhelm Pabst, an Austrian, glorified fraternity among workers. But his utopia did not last long. By the end of the film, political boundaries and secular antagonisms carried the day. GFFA distributed this film which was appreciated more by the critics than by the public.

12 and 15 percent. Yet Gaumont was still looking for its "paradise lost". In 1931, questioned about GFFA's projects, Léon's son, Louis Gaumont, declared: "They can be summed up in a few words—to try to regain the position we held in the world market at the beginning of 1914."

The gala re-opening of the Gaumont Palace on June 17, 1931, was not enough to silence the often malicious rumors that were making the rounds: "GFFA has laid off everyone from the director to the janitor." Such rumors proved to be idle gossip. At its board meeting of June 29, 1931, the company announced a profit of 9 million francs.

Relaunching GFFA

Theatrical exhibition business took off as the Gaumont Palace posted higher than expected profits. It seemed that Gaumont Franco Film Aubert had

Built in 1920 in Paris on the square of the same name, the Gambetta (below) was the first movie house conceived by an architect solely for cinematographic usage. Henri Sauvage created a real jewel of decorative art as applied to the cinema. In the 1930s, most of France's film houses were former theaters. In these buildings, which were not designed for film projection visibility remained a problem for those spectators seated far from the screen.

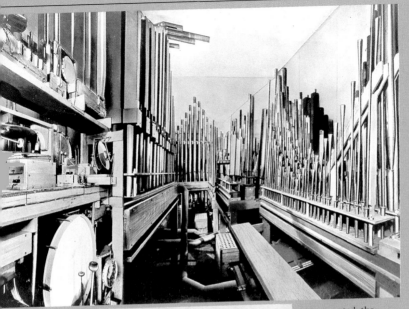

Renovated, the sumptuous Gaumont Palace now seated 6,000 and featured an acoustic ceiling adapted especially for sound. The theater counted two orchestras—one, symphonic, for playing overtures, and the second for the accompaniment of coming attractions. It was adorned with a cathedral-sized pipe organ (1,500 pipes) which rose from underneath the orchestra pit during intermission. Right: the control room complete with its own power generator just below the organ.

successfully made the transformation to sound. Indeed, even movie production had started up again: in June, 1932, four talkies were either in pre-production or being shot.

While on the surface things looked up, in fact, the financial situation was rather distressing. Debt was so high that the company was forced to cease certain activities and in nearly every sector cutbacks were imperative. In September, 1932, the new general manager, Paul Keim, announced harsh measures. The most drastic was the decision to halt production of

In the early 1930s Georges Milton, a rotund comedy actor and singer, became Bouboule, hero of two films directed by Léon Mathot: *La Bande à Bouboule* (1931) and *Bouboule Ier Roi Nègre* (left, 1933). His raciness and his talent earned him a pre-war success that equaled French actor Fernandel. Georges Milton was the highest paid actor in France: 3 million Francs per movie. The series of films, *Bouboule*, sold an average 236,000 tickets in week.

BOUBOULE Ier

Paul Keim, accompanied here by Georges Milton, tried to revive Gaumont. But he lacked the means to do so.

cameras. The investments required in order to remain competitive with the Americans and Germans were much too costly. Worse yet, GFFA's foreign-based outlets and offices—revived throughout the 1920's, and still not profitable—were "placed in mothballs". The poorly equipped and costly studios in Nice and Paris met with a similar fate: "for sale"

signs and lay-off notices. In exhibition, the head office took over programming from the individual movie house managers in a move to centralize operations.

Nor was production spared. Budgets were slashed after several films failed at the box office such as: Gaston Ravel's *Le Collier de la Reine*, René Barbéris' *Romance à l'Inconnue*, or Camille De Morlhon's *Roumanie, Terre d'Amour*. The company set a one-million-Francs-per-film limit on future productions. In addition, film-makers were forced to find partners with whom they could share financial risks.

The French movie industry finished 1932 on an almost euphoric note. So did GFFA which at the end of the year announced that it was preparing nine films—an impressive slate for the times. In addition, it noted that all were to be shot either at company studios in Nice or at the Buttes Chaumont. False optimism. Troubles were lurking in the shadows: the company's private owners were losing control to the State. Debt was about to go through the ceiling. Due to a series of capital increases subscribed to by shareholding banks such as Banque Nationale de

In 1933 Alexandre Volkoff shot *La Mille et Deuxième Nuit* for GFFA. Former baritone at the Moscow Opera, he was actor, script writer and studio head before becoming a film director in Russia. Overcome by the Russian Revolution, he left for Paris in 1920 with his troupe which included Mosjoukine — the star of most of his films. Hundreds of Russian technicians, artists and producers immigrated to France during this period. To promote this film, advertising material highlighted its numerous harem scenes (above) by using hand-colored stills.

Gaumont took care of the theater operators. Each film was accompanied with "an easy to do façade kit". For *Le Miracle des Loups* (Miracle of the Wolves), GFFA noted "the mysterious and dramatic allure" of its kit. "In the evenings, the wolves' eyes will turn transparent. Lit in yellow, this will create a striking effect."

Crédit (BNC), the French State had become GFFA's major shareholder. Henceforth, the State would dictate the company's policy.

Dark days ahead

The film industry seemed to be surviving the depression. Profits from exhibition had even increased. But production was another story. French films were struggling to compete with profitable American movies. GFFA's debt to the BNC rose to 200 million francs. The wild rumors began to surface again. Some said the Nice studios had been sold to Douglas Fairbanks, others that the Empain corporation had bought out GFFA.

In reality, starting in spring 1934, the depression caught up with the film industry. Shares of GFFA stock fell to seven francs—one-third their 1932 price. The company was in a constant state of reorganization. Eventually GFFA was turned over to a government committee—the Cinema Sub-Commission of the Chamber of Deputies' Finance Commission.

A clear-cut policy on how to run the debt-ridden GFFA would never emerge. It owed 320 million francs and the endless debate dragged on. Part of the reason for this was the sensitive political nature of the GFFA dossier. The government remained cautious. In May 1935 General Targe, presented as having a mandate from the Finance Minister, took over from Paul Keim. Meanwhile company debt

increased daily. It seemed that nothing could save Gaumont Franco Film Aubert. In September 1935, despite the efforts of the "great tactician", as the General Targe was called, the company declared bankruptcy and by the end of the month was put into compulsory liquidation.

L'Atalante (1934) Jean Vigo's masterpiece and last film was commercialized under the title: *Le Chaland qui Passe*. Under the pressure of theater operators, the film was mutilated and re-edited. To attract a larger audience a popular song was added, *Le Chaland qui Passe*, which was the origin of the movie title. Recently the film was restored to its original form.

The movie industry during the Popular Front strikes

Gaumont's bankruptcy followed close behind that of Pathé (February 1935) and caused consternation throughout the profession. In those years of fierce ideological struggles, the conservative press asked in May 1936: "Will GFFA and Pathé become the official State-run movie industry?" The position of the hard left CGT union, which was arguing for "complete nationalization" of the cinema, seemed to give credence to such an idea. Nationalization never took place but the debate raged on for years.

In spring 1936 strikes rapidly spread throughout

the country. Gaumont newsreels hushed up the event until June 5th when they announced that "the metal workers strike is over". Since early May the studios and the film developing laboratories were on strike. The Pathé-Cinéma studios in Joinville, the Francœur and Eclair studios in Epinay, and the GFFA studios at the Buttes Chaumont were shut down and occupied. From June 12th on, the strike movement assumed such proportions that the opening credits on Gaumont films carried the following statement: "Due to the strikes which have spread to the movie industry, *Eclair Journal*, *France Actualités Gaumont* and *Pathé Journal* are now unable to issue their respective newsreels and have joined together to present an edition of the week's events for their faithful clientele."

The Gaumont studios were in the forefront of the movement. GFFA's heavy debt to the State and the debate over nationalization certainly increased the strikers' resolve. Union policy called for the extension of the strike to all of GFFA's activities. Therefore GFFA's flagship theater, the Gaumont Palace, was among those sectors targeted. Led by

=ACTUALITES
LITES GAUMONT
PRÉSENTE
son
Journal N. 1

machinists and electricians, the employees of the prestigious theater joined the strike movement in the morning of June 4th. Box office receipts fell to zero and the financial losses were felt immediately. It took

The last silent newsreel was made in August 1931. The first talking newsreel *France Actualités Gaumont* appeared in October 1932. Gaumont named Germaine Dulac (left), a cinema professional, to head the new service. Suffragette, contributor to the feminist newspaper, *La Fronde*, Germaine Dulac founded in 1916 a production company, La Delia Film, run by her husband, Albert Dulac. Second woman film director—after Alice Guy—she fought many battles for esthetic improvements in theory as well as on the screen. But she never made the switch to talkies. In 1930 she gave up features for newsreels. She started at *Actualités Pathé* and then joined Gaumont where she stayed until 1940. Opposite: workers on strike during the Popular Front labor unrest, June 1936 (picture taken from a newsreel report).

Documentaries were programmed before the feature in every theater. They were treated as a completely separate but equal genre to the features. In the promotion package sent to movie house operators, documentaries received façade kits, press clippings and a mention in the ads. Thanks to documentaries exotic locations invaded the screen. Often their subjects dealt with a great expedition, civil or military. No continent was neglected. From the Basque country (*Au Pays des Basques*) to China (*Chine Eternelle*) and passing through Pamir (*Pamir, le Toit du Monde*), these documentaries were an invitation to discovery and day-dreaming as they romanticized explorers and adventurers. Released in 1931, *Sahara* was subtitled "In the mysterious regions of Hoggar with desert cargo". The poster's copy continued in the same vein: "unexplored regions", "perilous explorations" and "curious peoples". These somewhat facile eye-catching posters nevertheless did not take away from the high quality reporting contained in the documentaries.

only two days for the directors of the theater to give in to all of the strikers' demands. At 2:00 p.m., the ticket machines were turned back on. The strike hadn't lasted 48 hours! The Gaumont newsreel of June 19th briefly featured the end of the big strikes.

The road to war

In January 1938 attention was focused on what turned out to be a minor labor incident: the Tobis Studios—not part of Gaumont—went on strike. GFFA employees at Billancourt decided to join the movement but it went no further. While eyes were on this, a more ominous event was taking place unnoticed. In early spring 1938, a communiqué from the French Defense Department warned: location shots should not give away topographical information to the enemy!

Meanwhile General Targe resigned. His mission to put the company back on its feet had failed. His policy, which sought to turn the former Gaumont into a centralized organization "like a railroad company with uniformed civil servants", did not work. As the company waited for a new boss, its activities slowed to a snail's pace. A company administrator put it this way: "Only the Finance Minister can have projects! We can run no risks. So there will be no production. That means not even taking a share in a film. We are only allowed to operate the theaters."

A search went out for a powerful new owner who could breathe life back into GFFA. One was quickly found. In July 1938 Havas—a news and advertising agency with strong ties to the State—took control of GFFA. Havas' president, Léon Rénier, took on the same post at GFFA. He changed its name yet another time: Société Nouvelle des Etablissements Gaumont (SNEG). Under Rénier's helm some decisions were finally taken. To cut costs, distribution for France and North Africa were assigned to the De Rouvre Corporation. The Havas takeover riled up even more hostility from those who suspected the State wanted to turn Gaumont into a propaganda machine. Rénier responded by ignoring his critics. Another result of the Havas takeover was that it introduced Alain Poiré to Gaumont. Named to the post of secretary general by his grandfather, Rénier, in September 1938, Poiré would leave a permanent mark on the history of the company.

In September 1939, the declaration of war on Germany suddenly mooted the debate for or against the arrival of Havas in Gaumont. On June 5, 1940 while Gaumont newsreel number 23 was announcing measures taken against the Fifth Column and running a tribute to writer Charles Péguy— killed in action in 1914—Paris was bombarded.

Newsreels' popularity grew during the Thirties. Some theaters were even exclusively devoted to them. *France Actualités Gaumont* appeared weekly and was 15 minutes long. Each newsreel was shown on 300 screens and contained sports, political and high society news. Since each copy cost money to make, the newsreels were first screened in Paris in order to keep down distribution expenses. They were then sent out to the provinces, sometimes up to three months later.

Among the numerous newsreel cameramen working for Gaumont, Marcel Petiot held a longtime post covering the Elysées Palace — not an easy mission.

"In spite of the horror of the war and four years of German Occupation, the French film industry not only held on but it reached new heights of perfection."

The Daily Film Renter and Moving Pictures News, July 1945

CHAPTER III
FROM GERMAN OCCUPATION TO THE FIFTH REPUBLIC

The French had to ration goods due to the hardships of World War II and the German Occupation (right: a food ticket). Nevertheless they continued to go to the movies. In Lyon after the Liberation, the Royal Gaumont played Jacques Becker's film, *Les Rendez-vous de Juillet* (1949).

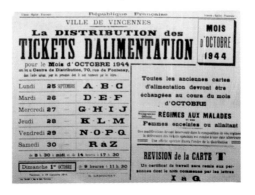

Against all odds the French movie industry, which had ceased operations with the German invasion, rapidly started up again. As early as June 19th, 20 Parisian theaters were re-opened. A week later, 60 had opened and a total of 100 by early July. The Rex and the Marignan were transformed into *Soldatenkino* for the German troops. On August 14th in Marseille, Marcel Pagnol resumed the shooting of *La Fille du Puisatier*.

At the end of October in Paris, two companies brought their directors together. Alfred Greven, appointed by Berlin to oversee the organization of French cinema, created the Continental. It would be the most prolific production company throughout the Occupation. Over on rue Caulaincourt, the Société Nouvelle des Etablissements Gaumont voted for an

increase of capital in order to continue its reorganization. In early 1941, a new increase of capital, which the state-controlled Havas refused to take part in, enabled Gaumont to avoid a German take-over. The Compagnie des Compteurs, later known as the Compteurs Schlumberger, bought into Gaumont.

The Gaumont daisy returns to the screen

SNEG reached an exclusive distribution agreement with Marcel Pagnol for both his catalog and for all films he would make in the next five years. In fact, it

"For *Le Journal Tombe à 5 Heures*, I chose a very competent director, Georges Lacombe (on our posters we wrote 'mise en scène'. The word 'réalisateur' [director] came later). Lacombe fell ill during pre-production. He was placed in quarantine in a hospital near the Montparnasse train station. That's where I went to see him. Our discussion took place with a glass window separating us. It wasn't a very convenient way to handle the thousand problems of a film shoot.**"**

Alain Poiré,
200 Films au Soleil

As soon as they got to Paris, the German Occupation troops requisitioned movie theaters which they turned into *Soldatenkinos*. The same measure was applied nearly all through the Occupied Zone, and later in 1943, in the former Free Zone. The Organizational Committee of the Cinematographic Industry required "a producer's card". In order to get one, Gaumont had to start-up a film immediately. This is how Alain Poiré produced his first film, *Le Journal...*: "I knew nothing about production (...). I was completely ignorant about everything that involved putting together a film—subjects, directors, actors, sets, shooting. But I had to start before February 1942."

bought out all his operations including his studios and sound laboratories in Marseille as well as his distribution services thus wiping clean his debts. This also prevented Continental from appropriating the Pagnol company. By the summer of 1941, the SNEG was back again in operation and was taking advantage of the German and Vichy government policy of relaunching the French cinema to appease the French people. SNEG used its theater circuit to measure the French demand for films. The gradual disappearance of collective outdoor activities and the halt of all British film imports in September of 1940, then of American films two years later, provided the most favorable conditions.

On January 23rd, 1942, Georges Lacombe shot the first scene of *Le Journal Tombe à 5*

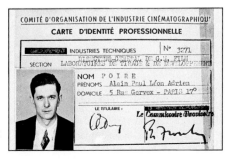

Heures. Gaumont was back in production. The movie premiered at the Colisée theater in May 1942. In the film Marie Déa, a high-spirited reporter, softens up Pierre Fresnay, a grouchy newspaperman. For the first time, Alain Poiré's name appeared in the credits. Nine other films were made during the Occupation. Each of them received funds from the Crédit National.

It should be mentioned that in August 1942—at the express request of the State—SNEG, along with Pathé and later Eclair, bought up a large block of the capital of *France Actualités* which, as of August, had become France's only newsreel service.

At the end of April 1942 in Toulon on the ocean-liner, *L'Océan*, Jean Dréville started filming *Les Cadets de l'Océan*. The film, which tells the story of the daily life aboard a Navy war instruction boat was eventually banned by the Occupation authorities because it was judged too nationalistic. After the Liberation its release was delayed until winter 1945. The censorship board considered that it portrayed young Frenchmen as being too frivolous: one sailor had a brief affair with a somewhat flighty young woman.

P roduced by the SNEG, *Vautrin*—adapted from Balzac's *Illusions perdues*—had an exceptional cast: Michel Simon (opposite, right) in the title role; Georges Marchal played Lucien de Rubempré (left); Madeleine Sologne was Esther. Others included Line Noro, Louis Seigner, Guillaume de Sax and Mouloudji. Released in January 1944, the film directed by Pierre Billon was a success. Trying to talk reason into Lucien de Rubempré who is passionately swept away by Esther, Michel Simon-Vautrin declares: "The throne trembles from its very foundations, Sir. Under such circumstances, it's better to have the services of a clever adventurer than the honesty of an imbecile!" Pronounced in 1944 during the Occupation, these words took on a political meaning.

The land of France is not for sale!

Things took a turn for the worse on January 10, 1943 but Société Nouvelle des Etablissements Gaumont had too much invested in production to pull the plug. The Organizational Committee of the Cinema Industry issued "decision 42" which—in the name of conserving electricity—ordered that French movie houses be limited to only 24 weekly showings. This decision was in part compensated by an increase of ticket prices decreed a month later by the same Committee. A decision applauded by the SNEG.

The company launched *Jeannou* by Léon Poirier and then in June, *Un Seul Amour* by Pierre Blanchar shortly followed by Pierre Billon's *Vautrin*. On the whole faithful to Balzac's work, *Vautrin* was made in late 1943 during the German Occupation : in Balzac's book, the character of Baron Nucingen was an Alsatian

J *eannou* (opposite) witnessed another political *double-entendre* of the period. Saturnin Fabre, a cheat who ends up in prison, learns from Marcelle Géniat that "the land of France cannot be sold—it can only be handed down".

With *Beauty and the Beast*— coproduced and distributed in October 1946 by Gaumont— Jean Cocteau directed his biggest box office success. For the role of the prince and the Beast, Cocteau had no hesitations: Jean Marais. For the Beauty, he hesitated. At first he thought of Josette Day, but she looked too much like a pin-up. Artistic director Christian Bérard took the initiative. He took Josette into the bathroom, ran water over her hair and made a chignon. She was chosen for the part. The filming didn't go smoothly. Cocteau suffered from allergy attacks and chronic headaches. Chief cameraman, Henri Alekan, accomplished his most brilliant lighting job—the final result was a masterpiece. Thanks to this film Gaumont received its first Louis Delluc award.

Jew. The movie version doesn't mention his background and only makes him out to be a dirty old man.

In 1944, events moved fast. The year began with the bombardment of the Renault factories in Boulogne-Billancourt. The air raid carried out by the Allied armies destroyed the nearby studios and killed 37 people. Other raids were soon to follow. Within a matter of weeks, 68 movie theaters would be wiped out by air raids. Yet, despite the dangers, French movie audiences kept growing and the Société Nouvelle des Etablissements Gaumont continued producing films.

The movie industry—liberated but in a pitiful state

German Occupation had been painful. All levels of society and all sectors of the economy had been affected. The movie industry was no exception. First of all there were the professionals. Many actors and technicians never returned from the war: the estimate of casualties totalled 240 dead or missing not including the unreleased prisoners of war. In that winter of 1944, Jean Cocteau was waiting for soldier Jean Marais' return—"still at the front"—so they could make *Beauty and the Beast*.

As for the theater business, bombs had wreaked great destruction. The large urban centers had suffered the most: 104 movie theaters were demolished in the Paris area alone. In Marseille, 27 had been hit and 16 totally destroyed. In all, 410 theaters throughout France had been damaged, representing 10 percent of the theaters equipped for 35 mm films.

Throughout the first winter of refound freedom, the lack of heat and the rationing of electricity remained a problem which was reflected at the box office. When the cold weather set in, receipts plummeted 40 percent in Paris and

Attendant in a reform school, Noël Noël pacifies one of the juvenile delinquents in *La Cage aux Rossignols*. Started in March 1944 the film wasn't released until September 1945. Also that year, several months after the Liberation, the French finally discovered Charlie Chaplin's parody of Hitler— *The Great Dictator*, which played at the Gaumont Palace.

20 percent in the provinces. For the year 1944 alone, Gaumont's turnover in Paris was half of its 1943 figure.

Hollywood go home!

Production as well suffered from the wounds of war. The lack of film stock disrupted the shooting of Yves Allégret's *Les Ames Qui Vivent* (*Les Démons de l'Aube*). The movie-making machine was bled dry just when the solitary confinement of the Occupation was ending. Hollywood came back strong. French production quickly suffered the consequences. For months, Gaumont limited its activity to simply renting out unoccupied studios.

Of all the sectors of the French economy, the movie industry was where objections to American presence would be the most vehement. A hard-fought battle followed, featuring two protagonists: Léon Blum and James Byrnes. The American argued for free trade; the Frenchman, well aware of Hollywood's appetite, wanted temporary protectionism. Under the banner of defending

In the days following the war, *Les Démons de l'Aube* told the story of heroic commandos. The picture quickly disappeared from the screens for lack of public interest.

French identity, the movie professionals were supported by the Gaullists and Communists in Parliament. Fernand Grenier, on behalf of the French Communist Party, hammered out his efficiently simple declarations before the National Assembly: "There are far too many French young people who know Gary Cooper but who are unaware of Guynemer. The French movie industry must be rescued!"

Optimism came back to the screen as witnessed by Jacques Becker's *Antoine et Antoinette* (opposite). Triumphant success. In less than nine months foreign sales covered half of production cost. Impressive considering that the film was expensive. Shooting lasted 22 weeks in the

FESTIVAL DU FILM CANNES

GRAND PRIX D'HONNEUR
CATÉGORIE : FILMS PSYCHOLOGIQUES ET D'AMOUR
DÉCERNÉ A *Jacques Becker*
POUR LE FILM *Antoine et Antoinette*
France

1947

"Antoine et Antoinette"—just a simple love story

In this context Gaumont signed and co-signed such fine works as *La Cage aux Rossignols* by Jean Dréville and especially *Antoine et Antoinette* by Jacques Becker, which started shooting in 1946. Unlike René Clément's recently released *La Bataille du Rail* (first prize at the Cannes Film Festival), Becker's movie didn't refer to the great battles of the past or present. It even left out the strikes which were then disrupting the country. The author wanted to produce "just a simple love story in working class Paris".

The film was a box office success. Thanks to its foreign sales and its triumph in France, *Antoine et Antoinette* allowed those at Gaumont who argued for production to

studio, the longest of the year. It received seven prizes at the 1947 Cannes festival. Opposite: a humorous drawing excerpted from an ad for *Antoine et Antoinette*. The CPLF (Compagnie Parisienne de Location de Films) was a distribution company bought out by the SNEG. The cigar underscored the company's prosperity.

regain their confidence. In 1947 when the "agony of the French movie industry" was a regular topic of discussion, the success of *Antoine et Antoinette* helped to relieve the feelings of pessimism in the heart of the illustrious house of Gaumont.

In the following years, Gaumont produced relatively few films but all were quality productions such as *Croisière pour l'Inconnue* by Pierre Montazel in 1947. The following years Gaumont released Jean Dréville's *Les Casse-pieds*, Jacques Becker's *Les Rendez-vous de Juillet* and Henri Calef's *La Souricière* and *L'Invité du Mardi*.

"Caroline Chérie", a scent of scandal

Monseigneur Gerbier was undoubtedly right when at the 1953 release of *Un Caprice de Caroline Chérie*, he chastized the "scandalous speculation on vice". It

The response to *Un Caprice de Caroline Chérie* (1953, opposite) was nearly unanimous—aside from some hostile reactions such as congressman Bouxom who thought the film should've been censored. The public was fascinated by the chassé-croisé love-life of Martine Carol-Caroline de Bièvres and Jacques Dacqmine-Gaston de Salanches. *Un Caprice* had a twelve week exclusive run and made Martine Carol a star. Her name alone brought in 117 million Francs per

is true that Gaumont took full advantage of Martine Carol's shapely derrière. The actress was as generous with her body as she had been three years earlier in *Caroline Chérie*, the first in the series and the year's biggest moneymaker. Gaumont was wringing its hands over the results: after less than seven months the film had gone into profit.

What was the reason for this amazing success? Was it the public's homage to the first French film shot in Technicolor? That was very unlikely. How about an infatuation with Martine Carol who was then at the height of her popularity? That was more probable. There could well have been a more titillating reason for this success, namely one aspect of the film's originality as compared with contemporary American movies. As rich as they were

film. Impressed by the success of *Un Caprice* , Gaumont produced *The Son of Caroline Chérie*. The action took place this time in Napoleonic Spain with Brigitte Bardot in the lead role—it was her first Gaumont film.

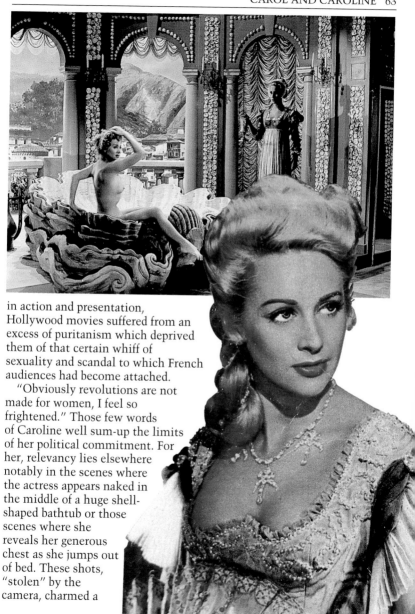

in action and presentation, Hollywood movies suffered from an excess of puritanism which deprived them of that certain whiff of sexuality and scandal to which French audiences had become attached.

"Obviously revolutions are not made for women, I feel so frightened." Those few words of Caroline well sum-up the limits of her political commitment. For her, relevancy lies elsewhere notably in the scenes where the actress appears naked in the middle of a huge shell-shaped bathtub or those scenes where she reveals her generous chest as she jumps out of bed. These shots, "stolen" by the camera, charmed a

public which would soon be ready for the torrid eroticism of the sixties.

The Gaumont monopoly

While Gaumont was joining its name to those of Martine Carol or Sacha Guitry, who starred in five Gaumont films, an enormous game of monopoly was going on behind the public's back. From the very first days of the French Liberation, the company well-understood that if it didn't give the public a total show it wouldn't maintain its loyalty. The pleasure of the eye should be accompanied by a maximum of auditory and esthetic comforts. Gaumont was aiming at justifying its ticket prices which were higher than its neighborhood competitors. The company also

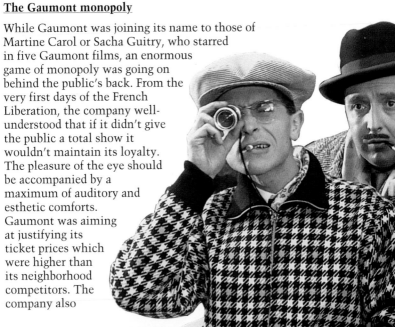

understood in the early 1960's that another latent public existed: "An extra clientele which can be recruited from among our fellow citizens, too numerous to our liking, who only go to the movies rarely because of a lack of comfort and show."

The company then went on a buying and selling spree while at the same time pursuing a renovation campaign under the leadership of architect Georges Peynet. This policy got results.

Gaumont successfully held its own during an industry-wide box office slump which lasted the decade— sometimes reaching a 10% annual drop in receipts.

Thanks to the quality of its theaters and its programming policy, Gaumont's tickets held relatively steady.

The theater of the Casino Municipal in Nice (above, the model) was entirely refurbished by architect H. Chatelain.

Les Trois Font la Paire (opposite, Darry Cowl) was Sacha Guitry's last film. "A work where humor and disenchantment make an astonishing cocktail [...] a cynical testament to humanity, justice, women [...]. Because it is just that—a testament. Sacha knew that he couldn't direct this film." (Alain Poiré). In fact, Guitry was bed-ridden with diabetes. He gave instructions from his bedside.

"**F**ashion is beginning to appear. Everything is short-lived. Playing commercials during intermission is imposing a new rite which has been completely sanctioned by the public. Movie theaters must change. The public is gentrifying. They are more educated and they are making more choices."

Maurice Bessy,
Le Film Français, October 1958

CHAPTER IV
FROM SCOOTERS TO MULTIPLEXES

Sign of the times, *Les Tontons Flingueurs* (left, 1963) bemoans the drop in prostitution at the hands of television. The cinema itself has to deal with the small screen. Opposite: the Evry complex opened from 10 a.m. to 2 a.m.

In the movie theaters, newsreels were used to promote the films. Jean Jay (opposite, center, with Alain Poiré and his wife, and Michèle Morgan) started to work at *France Actualités* in 1934; he was then the head of *Gaumont Actualités* from the end of World War II to 1969.

Cannes June 1959 : the public at the 12th edition of the International Festival of Film discovered a revolutionary style from a handful of auteurs—all virtual unknowns: Marcel Camus, Alain Resnais, Claude Chabrol and François Truffaut. The latter would receive the Golden Palm for *Les Quatre Cents Coups* (*The Four Hundred Blows*).

The torment of the 1960's

This event didn't go unnoticed at Gaumont. These directors had been making their out-of-the-ordinary films for the last two years. Nevertheless Gaumont kept its reserve. It wanted to see what effect the films would have on the box office. So far, most of them had been disappointing. Mass audiences go for proven formulas—adventure, action, comedy. And Gaumont had survived for all these years thanks to these kinds of movies. The same conclusion was made by Gaumont's distribution department which had been experiencing tremendous success with *Ben Hur* and *Spartacus*. New Wave films were hard to commercialize. The State still complained about sex and juvenile crime on the screen and slapped them with R ratings (no one under 18). Sometimes it banned the film outright. In any case commercial

disaster was always a possibility. So Gaumont continued to pursue its market with young and not so young directors such as Roger Vadim (*Le Vice et la Vertu*, 1961), Edouard Molinaro (*Un Témoin dans la Ville*), Robert Hossein (*La Nuit des Espions*, 1959) and Henri Decoin (*Tendre et Violente Elisabeth*). Gaumont financed Claude Autant-Lara's *Le Comte de Monte Cristo* rather than his *Les Régates de San Francisco* which local authorities censored.

Gaumont SAB was a Belgian subsidiary totally controlled by the French, whose main activity was distributing Gaumont films (below) and others in Belgium, until 1992.

Sharing the costs

Nevertheless Gaumont kept its ears to the ground. In 1961 it relaunched production of shorts and educational films which it programmed prior to features. At the same time it pursued a complementary objective: to share production expenses. Indeed prices were soaring—up 45% between 1958 and 1961, far outpacing box office receipts. Therefore Gaumont decided to find partners with whom it could split these costs. In February 1962, Alain Poiré took control of a new subsidiary, Gaumont International. In addition, Gaumont brought back to use an old practice : it signed three year contracts with directors such as Hossein and André Cayatte, and with screen writers such as Michel Audiard. And in order to share costs, Gaumont coproduced in Italy *Les Lanciers Noirs* (1962) and *Le Procès des Doges* (1963). The creation of Gaumont Italiana in 1964 capped Gaumont's Italian incursion.

Prince's — hotel 90, av. Elisabeth & av. Lippens TEL. 61302 - KNOKKE

Vrijdag / Vendredi 15 tot maan / au lundi 18 juni om / juin à 9 u. h.

Zondag namid. vert. / Dimanche matinées 3 & 5.30 u. h.

Enfants non admis   Kinders niet toegelaten

GAUMONT présente une CO-PRODUCTION ELOI FILMS · GAUMONT ACTUALITÉS · S.N.E. GAUMONT

ANOUK AIMÉE
JACQUES DACQMINE

QUAI NOTRE DAME

UN FILM DE
JACQUES BERTHIER
D'APRÈS LE ROMAN DE
DOMINIQUE ROLLIN "ELOI" ÉDITIONS DENOËL
avec
CHRISTIAN PEZEY
CHRISTIAN ALERS
GENEVIÈVE FONTANEL, LISETTE JAMBEL
and
PATRICIA GOZZI

LIEVE VROUWEKADE ©

In 1961, Claude Autant-Lara filmed the 25th version of *The Count of Monte Cristo* (left, Louis Jourdan-Edmond Dantès during a break). That year, France had 2.5 million TV sets and the most serious estimates put the saturation point at seven million.

The cathodic menace

The big news of the period was television. Gaumont had an exceptionally large number of managers who held degrees from France's top engineering schools. So from TV's beginning they foresaw the possible ways in which they could work with the small screen. In 1953, Gaumont took shares in the Société pour la Télédiffusion then in the Société Marocaine de Radio Télédiffusion— appropriate measures considering that from 1956 the spread of the tube would begin eating into box office results. In 1960 Gaumont took part in a new company set-up to study pay television. Its familiarity with the technical culture as well as its shareholding links with the Compagnie des Compteurs were the background reasons why it signed on Dassault Electronique in 1967 so it could equip its theater circuit to project television rebroadcasts of the winter Olympics in Grenoble. Several years later, Dassault took a ten percent stake of Gaumont and became its third largest shareholder.

Among all of France's film production companies, Gaumont was undoubtedly the most impassioned for the small screen. This did not prevent it, however, from regularly criticizing the State TV monopoly— ORTF—and the low prices it paid for the broadcast rights of its films.

One direct consequence of the coming of

As television gained territory, the movie industry tried to cash in. The Bosquet Gaumont was the first theater equipped to rebroadcast TV programs on the big screen. In 1960, it showed the Rome Olympics live. Eleven million households had TV by 1969. Two years before technical needs linked to the theaters brought together Gaumont and Dassault (top right, Marcel Dassault). In 1980 Gaumont newsreels was victim of television's onslaught, as all other newsreels.

TV was the slow but sure death of the newsreel. Too expensive, too slow journalistically. In 1969, Actualités Gaumont absorbed its rival Actualités Eclair. They surprisingly survived several more years outlasting Pathé Actualités. It took many years for the French public to embrace television, unlike its wildfire spread in the US and the UK. Things have come full circle—

Better to acquit two guilty parties than to convict an innocent one. In *Le Glaive et la Balance* (1963), André Cayatte directed a courtroom drama and cinematographic plea which was highly criticized by the New Wave. Center, the accused: A. Perkins, J.C. Brialy and R. Salvatori.

today Gaumont sells its newsreels archives to television.

Pleasing a young audience

At the height of the Fifth Republic—mid 1960's— France underwent an unprecedented economic and social transformation. The French went on a buying frenzy: cars, refrigerators, scooters... and televisions. The movie industry was deeply affected. In order to finance this spending, consumers cutback their entertainment budget. This meant going less to the movies. Gaumont anticipated the drop. Thanks to its modernized circuit it was able to stave off a massive decrease in receipts.

And the films? Already in 1958, Alain Poiré evoked the rejuvenation of the movie-going public: "Television's success should incite us to produce for a young public—those who go out even if their parents stay at home to watch television. We should target this audience." In fact, the tastes and the

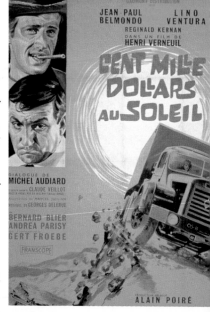

With newly found economic riches, the French began to lose their working class roots. Nevertheless Michel Audiard (opposite center with Mireille Darc and Alain Poiré) maintained his success based on slangy, street-wise dialogue. He wrote dialogue for *Cent Mille Dollars au Soleil* (1963), then for *Les Barbouzes*, as well as for many others.

habits of the time had all changed. And through these turbulent times, Gaumont succeeded in making films which stayed in step with audiences even with the widest of tastes. During the next 15 years, its yearly batting average was quite impressive: for every six films it made per year, it scored with two hits. Among the more notable titles: *Un Taxi pour Tobrouk* (1961), *Les Tontons Flingueurs* (1963), *Les Barbouzes* (1963), *Cent Mille Dollars au Soleil* (1963), the series of *Fantômas*. Yves Robert, Michel Audiard, Georges Lautner, Gérard Oury and Edouard Molinaro are among those who helped Gaumont bridge the generation gap.

The end of the Sixties started the trend of shortened runs in the theaters. The public would rush to a film in its opening weeks. But attendance would then rapidly drop off. This forced distributors to increase the number of theaters and the number of prints in order to get the maximum return out of the opening weeks. In 1966, Gaumont and Pathé signed a theater programming accord that the rest of the profession applauded. The new circuit which emerged

Cent Mille Dollars au Soleil was filmed in black and white in the middle of the color boom—at the American coproducer's demand. It was colorized for television in the 1990's.

Fifty years after the serials of Feuillade, *Fantômas* was brought back to the screen this time under the guise of Jean Marais. In comparison with the original, the remake was less cruel and funnier thanks to the rubber-face grimaces of comic Louis de Funès as the constantly ridiculed Commissaire Juve. Released December 4, 1964, it sold 400,000 tickets during its show case twelve week run. In the end, it sold 4 million. Two sequels followed: *Fantômas se Déchaîne*, 1965, and *Fantômas contre Scotland Yard*, 1967.

Francis Veber teamed with Yves Robert in 1972. The film was *Le Grand Blond avec une Chaussure Noire*. The plot evolved around a hapless violinist manipulated by French secret service agents. Theater operators didn't believe in it, yet Pierre Richard (opposite) was a triumph on the screen. The film's success also made Weston very happy: the shoe manufacturing company saw its sales take off thanks to the movie. Two years later, the sequel: *Le Retour du Grand Blond*.

from that agreement counted 150 theaters and 120,000 seats and represented an annual turnover of 150 million French Francs. Reshaped several times, the Pathé-Gaumont pact lasted until 1982.

The late Gaumont Palace

The year 1967 ended on a high note with *Oscar* and *Les Risques du Métier*. Gaumont looked forward to the new year. Then came May 68: widespread strikes and student unrest crippled the country. In fact Gaumont made it through that tumultuous month quite well. Its theaters remained opened and full thanks to a television strike. Only the production machine was affected. The strikes shut down the filming of *Le Cerveau* and also resulted in salary increases. Gaumont learned a business lesson through all

this: it must diversify. It must divide its large theaters into smaller units, and above all, modernize. In 1969, it put into service its first automatic projection booths which were then used starting in 1971 in the multiplexes. The result was immediate: ticket sales rose nine percent the first year. But down came the Gaumont Palace. Costly renovations were compensated by the success of its films: *Il Etait une Fois un Flic, Le Grand Blond Avec une Chaussure Noire* and *Mais Où Est donc Passée la 7ᵉ Compagnie?*

In the history of Gaumont, 1974-75 were key years. It wasn't because of the construction of a complex in Evry, in the suburbs of Paris—five screens, bowling alley and disco—nor the box office success of *La Gifle* and *Le Retour du Grand Blond*. The actual reason was less visible at the time. The ownership and

management of the company had completely changed. Jean Le Duc, chairman 1941-71, died that year. In 1975 his successor, Roger Sallard, was replaced when Nicolas Seydoux acquired the majority control of Gaumont and became chairman and chief executive officer.

In 1973 the French economy was booming at 5% annual increase and the Renault R5 sold for 10,960 Francs ($2,000). Paris underwent a major face-lift: the city's historic marketplace, Les Halles, was demolished as was the Gaumont Palace. The latter represented 7,000 square feet of real estate which was sold for 35 million Francs. In place, an architectural project which grouped a hotel and a shopping gallery was supposed "to revolutionize the cul-de-sac at Place Clichy". The Palace's last poster had been for a John Wayne movie. The most prestigious movies had been screened there: *The Great Dictator* attracted 585,000 spectators in nine weeks; *Ben Hur* which ran for nine months...

Le Cerveau (1969) or how two clever crooks try to hold-up a postal train. As complicated as the robbery, the script succeeded in marrying Jean-Paul Belmondo and Bourvil (opposite) with David Niven and Eli Wallach.

"The cinema is a regime of universal suffrage. I respect the public's choice. It is usually the same spectators who go to see very different types of films. I believe it's essential that we preserve this variety but keep in mind the relationship between a film's potential and its cost."

Nicolas Seydoux,
1984

CHAPTER V
THE DAISY AT ONE-HUNDRED

Enigmatic and passionate, the stars of *The Big Blue* (1988) and *Betty Blue* (1986; opposite, Béatrice Dalle) kindled a widespread enthusiasm. Luc Besson and Jean-Jacques Beineix directed these cult films of the new decade. They proved that tragedy can still be successful.

Jewel of the French cinema in Latin America, Gaumont do Brazil, created in 1978, put together an 18-theater circuit in Rio and Sao Paulo. In eight years, the company distributed 400 films, principally art movies, according to Brazilian critics. The Brazilian subsidiary employed nearly 300 persons. In April 1985 its activities stopped. Four months earlier, the country's president had called for the complete nationalization of the Brazilian cinema. Gaumont's circuit was sold to a company which already owned 60 theaters. The battle against foreign multinationals did not displease everyone.

Gaumont's new chairman and chief executive officer Nicolas Seydoux, 35, worked for several years in New York at the investment bank, Morgan Stanley & Co. His experience in the US helped shape his policy at Gaumont. He was convinced that the film company had to diversify even further and above all it had to move into the foreign arena so it could lower its dependence on the French domestic market. His new assistant managing director, Daniel Toscan du Plantier, an ad agency executive, seconded Seydoux's planetary ambitions.

The world dream

At the end of 1977, Gaumont's top brass embarked on a study trip to Beijing and Rio de Janeiro with the obligatory stop in Hollywood. On their return, the battle plan started to take shape. Gaumont signed alliances—the main one with American major studio Fox whose films Gaumont would distribute in France. In 1978, Gaumont went on the offensive, creating companies in two reputed cinephile countries—Italy and Brazil: Gaumont do Brasil, Gaumont Italia and Opera Film (Italy). Their brief was to distribute and/or produce films. In the US, Gaumont Inc. was founded and Triumph Films in association with Columbia. Gaumont also took a 50 % stake in Téléfrance, a US cable channel which broadcast primarily French-made programs in French. The following year a third Italian company was created and in New York Gaumont launched Twin Studio to manage its US movie theaters.

The idea was to create an efficient and profitable distribution network. As producer, Gaumont had a hard time standing by while its films were exploited by third parties. For example: *Cousin, Cousine* released in 1975, was a great success in the US but brought no financial rewards for Gaumont. The company's new international distribution network should have rectified that allowing Gaumont to control the film from production to sales. A classic industrial practice.

For ten years Nicolas Seydoux and Daniel Toscan du Plantier (below) worked together as a team. Toscan said of his former boss: "Here is a loyal, rational, well-balanced, kind, lucid, hard-working and prudent man. The reader is authorized to add all other available respectable adjectives." Toscan maliciously added: "But what would a man as nice as him be doing in the business if he weren't the craziest of us all."

The cinema more than just entertainment

While Gaumont was expanding internationally, Toscan du Plantier installed a new production policy. The sign of the times was unmistakable: films weren't only a form of simple entertainment. So without abandoning its productions aimed at a wide mass audience, Gaumont opened up its production to another type of movie: a cinema made by different types of auteurs coming from different cultural horizons. This new policy allowed Gaumont to cover the spectrum of audience tastes.

The turning point came with the successful film version of opera *Don Giovanni* by Joseph Losey in 1979. After the theaters, moviegoers raided record shops for the sound track. Taking note, Gaumont purchased record label Erato, so it could better control the distribution of film music. In the same vein, Gaumont produced *Parsifal* by German director Hans-Jurgen Syberberg (1982) and Francesco Rosi's *Carmen* (1984)

Gérard Depardieu and Isabelle Huppert in 1980 played in *Loulou*, Maurice Pialat's first film for Gaumont. The story is awash in a moist and tense ambience where the main characters are constantly looking to find themselves.

starring a racy Julia Migenes Johnson. Gaumont also distributed *La Traviata* by Italian director Francesco Zeffirelli.

Concurrently, Toscan hunted cinema's great international auteurs. Gaumont believed that it alone could offer these renowned film directors a hospitality equal to their genius. Those invited were Ingmar Bergman, Federico Fellini, Francesco Rosi, Michelangelo Antonioni, Ettore Scola, Luigi Comencini, Andrzej Wajda, Andrei Tarkovski and many others who received carte blanche. The Swedish director shot his "testament" *Fanny and Alexander* (1983), a family saga inspired by his childhood. Fellini directed two of his last great works: *City of Women* (1980) and *And the Ship Sails on* (1984), a strange funeral ceremony. Tarkovski made *Nostalghia* (1983) in Italy, and Wajda created *Danton* (1982) played by Gérard Depardieu and Wojcieh Pszoniak as Maximilien Robespierre.

On the initiative of Daniel Toscan du Plantier, Gaumont opened up to foreign directors who were neglected by French producers. "France should be the world leader of non-American cinema." In 1983, Tarkovski—Gaumont had distributed *Stalker* four years earlier—directed *Nostalghia*. The shoot was extremely difficult considering Tarkovski's illness and the two KGB agents who were constantly at his side.

In the feverish Seventies, Gaumont launched into musical productions. Gaumont Musique prospected French pop stars (opposite, album cover of Jacques Dutronc's *C'est pas du Bronze*, 1982) while Erato, a prestigious record label, was more traditional.

A catalog for all types of audiences

From psychological drama to filmed opera, Gaumont covered the gamut in the Seventies. In 1974, it produced *La Gifle*, by Claude Pinoteau—the film which launched the career of Isabelle Adjani (opposite with her screen father, Lino Ventura). Five years later, Gaumont produced *Don Giovanni* directed by Joseph Losey (below, left: Kiri Te Kanawa) and started a genre destined for a completely different type of audience: the opera-film. Continuing in the same vein, the company produced *Carmen* by Francesco Rosi in 1984. The film was a great success, attracting 2 million spectators in France. More than 100,000 soundtracks were sold. The producer, Patrice Ledoux, made his mark by bringing the film in on time and on budget. The same year the French discovered *Marche à l'Ombre* (produced by Christian Fechner), the first film by Michel Blanc, a comic who made his fame with a Parisian theater troupe. Blanc invented a character —a hypochondriac loser who desperately sought a partner to sleep with. Gaumont is producing another of his films in 1994—*Grosse Fatigue*.

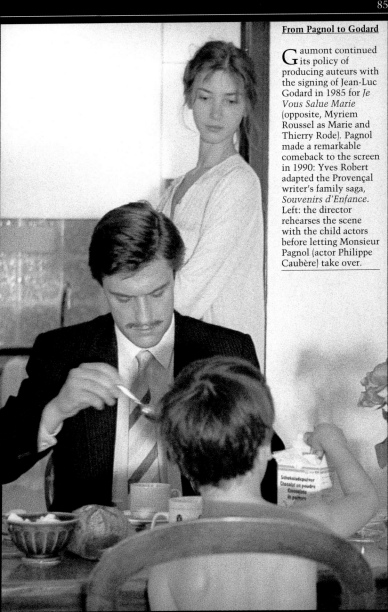

From Pagnol to Godard

Gaumont continued its policy of producing auteurs with the signing of Jean-Luc Godard in 1985 for *Je Vous Salue Marie* (opposite, Myriem Roussel as Marie and Thierry Rode). Pagnol made a remarkable comeback to the screen in 1990: Yves Robert adapted the Provençal writer's family saga, *Souvenirs d'Enfance*. Left: the director rehearses the scene with the child actors before letting Monsieur Pagnol (actor Philippe Caubère) take over.

Gaumont also went into the publishing business when it bought publishing house Editions Ramsay and weekly news magazine, *Le Point*. A new company Edivisuel was created between publishing house Gallimard and Gaumont to commercialize the rights of the Gallimard library.

Audacious and original, the policy of Toscan du Plantier nevertheless ran aground faced with the realities of the marketplace. The public stayed away from those prestigious quality films. In fact on several fronts the bottom line worsened.

A time for retrenching

The first alert came in 1981. The diverse Italian activities suffered from the inertia of local government. The different companies were regrouped

under one banner. But money kept on pouring out. Even though Gaumont owned a first-class theater circuit of 33 houses, the Italian market was confronted with enormous problems. For instance, it was impossible to obtain local authorization to create multiplexes, to adapt them to the new tastes of the audience. Worse, the anarchic development of private television suddenly plunged the business into depression—when just a few years earlier it was prospering. In 1983 Gaumont threw in the towel. It subleased its studios and stopped all Italian production. In the meantime, on the American front, Téléfrance was liquidated in

With *And the Ship Sails on*, Fellini assures the transition of the opera-film to a film about opera. As the Italian director put it, the film treats "certain worrisome problems such as the excess of information, information from the mass media which are completely disengaged from responsibility like a river of lava which covers everything, [...] which makes it so that we no longer have a direct knowledge of the world or life, and that we finish by only knowing things through the milky glass eye of television."

History is an important subject for Italian directors. *La Nuit de Varennes* by Ettore Scola brought together a perfect international cast. In the photo: surrounding Casanova (Marcello Mastroianni), the countess Sophie de la Borde (Hanna Schygulla), madame Adelaïde Gagnon (Andréa Ferreol), the writer Thomas Paine (Harvey Keitel) and Nicolas Restif de la Bretonne (Jean-Louis Barrault). During the shooting, Scola was armed with a black, felt-tip pen and scribbled constantly in notebooks which he would then slip into his jacket. He left a great quantity of sketches of Casanova (below) as well as the king, the queen and others.

September 1983: the 600,000 cable fans of French programs presented too small of an advertising base even for French companies.

In 1984, Gaumont's organizational chart no longer mentioned Brazil. Moreover the country's new president, José Sarney, embarked on a "Brazilization" of the movie industry. Gaumont do Brasil with its 18 theaters and 300 employees closed its doors the following year.

Record label Erato was sold in June 1985. Ramsay's losses were temporarily halted thanks to the success of *La*

Bicyclette Bleue by Régine Desforges (6.5 million copies sold). But in 1989 Gaumont was forced to sell the publishing company. Only news magazine *Le Point* stayed in the group just until 1993. All these operations, including the sale of its theater Colisée on the Champs Elysées, brought in much needed cash.

Gaumont gave up its dreams of reconstituting its international empire. Outside of neighboring Belgium where the firm still operates and New York where it has six theaters in association with Daniel Talbot, Gaumont has retrenched within the French borders.

The daisy and the small screen

In 1985 the French government asked Gaumont to get involved with the launching of a sixth television channel, TV6. Thus Gaumont became partners with Publicis, France's second largest ad agency. The first, Havas (former Gaumont owner), is shareholder in pay television service Canal Plus. Programs started on March 1, 1986. They were mostly music clips aimed at a young audience. Despite its success, the channel ceased operations one year later due to politics. TV6 became M6 without Gaumont. The venture left Gaumont with 110 million French Francs in losses.

"Bad luck exists. There are those who are born under a black cloud just as there are others who are born lucky. That's all there is to it." The eternal bad luck kid, Pierre Richard found himself confronted with a skeptical Gérard Depardieu in Francis Veber's hit comedy, *La Chèvre* (1981). In 1986 the same team shot another comedy success, *Les Fugitifs*. Below: the director and his two actors taking a break during the shooting of *La Chèvre*.

"We're no longer living in the Sixties when television was considered by the cinema as the enemy or even the devil", noted Nicolas Seydoux in 1987. For several years, sales of made-for-TV productions multiplied. Among the latest: the series *Highlander* (opposite: Adrian Paul who succeeded Christophe Lambert in the leading role) was presold to 60 foreign TV channels. Gaumont, in association with the Brizzi brothers, jumped back into animation. *Astérix et la Surprise de César* (below) was made in Paris from April 1984 to October 1985 with the help of 200 artists and technicians. Gaumont produced three other *Astérix* and a *Lucky Luke* which was adapted for television.

Gaumont and television have not always had conflicts. The company produces for television: it proposes programs which, if accepted, it partially prefinances. Already in the 1970's, Gaumont created with ORTF (state-run television) several series such as *Paul Gauguin*, *Les Dossiers Noirs* and *L'Inventaire des Campagnes*. Television allowed Gaumont to discover talents which later could move into features. Unfortunately, its early television production activities lost money. Gaumont pulled the plug.

Gaumont made a reappearance in television in the mid-1980's as France created three new private channels (including the ill-fated TV6). The situation had completely changed: more channels meant more competition. Program prices rose dramatically. In 1992 a newly created company, Gaumont Télévision (100% Gaumont) developed an ambitious slate of television production which enjoys an international success with shows such as

A ttendance dropped 40 % from 1982 to 1989. In this context, theater owners were forced to adapt to the new demands of the consumer. One year after buying the Kinopanorama in 1991, Gaumont opened the Grand Ecran (Giant Screen) on the Place d'Italie (in Paris). The complex was the first new building of a movie house since 1985. It contains a main theater of 685 seats with a screen of 24 x 10 meters and two smaller theaters of 100 seats. All three are equipped with Dolby sound. Films aren't the complex's only activities. To boost revenues, its rooms are used for seminars.

Highlander. One of the major success of Gaumont Télévision was a French documentary directed by the famous volcanologist Haroun Tazieff, *Le Feu de la Terre* («The fire of earth»).

Sales of films to television has been a booming business since the mid-1980's. On November 4, 1984, Canal Plus "the cinema channel" went on the air with *L'As des As* directed by Gérard Oury and produced by Gaumont. In the ten year period 1983-1992 sales revenues to television increased four-fold.

Television also needs archive material. Sales to generalist channels as well as thematic ones have allowed Cinémathèque Gaumont to increase the sales of its library of one thousand hours of programs. The advent of video has also increased sales of its library.

Multiplexes and giant screens

During the 1980's Gaumont continued its policy of acquiring and modernizing theaters in the large cities. It bought the real estate when possible. When feasible, it increased the number of screens. Starting in 1985, in Rouen, Bordeaux and Paris, the larger theaters were systematically equipped with big screens measuring at least 14 meters in width and

baptized Gaumontrama. Today each renovated multiplex has a Gaumontrama screen. Gaumont also installed other modern techniques such as reservation by telephone, payment by credit card and subscription cards. More than ever Gaumont oriented its policy towards making its theaters as comfortable as possible. Its circuit of 212 theaters welcomed some 17 million moviegoers in 1993 representing 14% of the French box office total with only 5% of the theaters. The inauguration of Gaumont Grand Ecran in Paris in June 1992 was the high point in the company's modernization strategy.

Distribution—less known by the public —plays a key role in the company's bottom line. An agreement signed in January 1992 with Walt Disney has made Gaumont the leading distributor in France, assuring the theater operators of a constant pipeline of top quality films. Gaumont also leads the market in home video distribution thanks to its co-venture with Columbia Tristar.

The Gaumont Ambassade—50 Avenue des Champs Elysées—was built on land bought in 1958 by architect George Peynet. The first theater was inaugurated in September 1959 by *La Jument Verte*. During the years, it grew larger to the detriment of a clothing shop and then a Chinese restaurant. Transformed into a five screen multiplex in 1981, it was enriched with a giant screen, Gaumontrama, and an additional 400 seats theater. By 1993 it had seven screens.

Awfully successful

Having started at Gaumont in 1938, Alain Poiré has remained a constant and intelligent force in the production of the company's stable: mainstream films. Allying laughter with emotion, he has pursued his policy of making eclectic and popular movies. Among his biggest successes was *La Boum* in 1980 which was considered a social phenomenon. Lead actress, Sophie Marceau, 13 1/2, received 160,000 letters. The sequel, *La Boum 2*, two years later proved that the first one was no fluke.

Then came *L'As des As* (1982) where delirious Jean-Paul Belmondo criss-crossed Bavaria, Germany, during the Nazi period. The day it opened, it sold a phenomenal 73,000 tickets in Paris. Also successful were comedies with Pierre Richard, the eternal screen victim comic unveiled in the 1972 hit *Le Grand Blond avec une Chaussure Noire*. His subsequent hits included *Le Coup du Parapluie* (1980) and *La Chèvre* (1981) co-starring Gérard Depardieu.

It is no coincidence that Alain Poiré would turn to the writings of the late Marcel Pagnol, the famed writer and director who was Poiré's close friend. The results were *My Father's Glory* and *My Mother's Castle* in

A star in France, Sophie Marceau is also a star in Japan (opposite: a ticket for *La Boum*). Other artists of international fame, Jean-Jacques Beineix (above left) and Luc Besson (below right) are two of the Gaumont auteurs of the Eighties. Left: Nicolas Seydoux and Patrice Ledoux pose in front of the mock-up for film poster of *The Big Blue*.

"The sun played an important role: in the beginning, I wanted to call my film 'Life-time Bra'. Finally it was the sun that won—the sun of Marseille with the sea in the background and on the other side, Africa, where friends of mine were born." After having worked forty years with Bernard Blier, Gaumont associated with his son, Bertrand: an exacting author, difficult to classify, who places himself "in the opposition at all costs", because if not, "you become an official director". The film was called *Un, Deux, Trois, Soleil* (*One, Two, Three, Sun*).

1990 both based on Pagnol's *Childhood Souvenirs*. In producing them Poiré had taken a double risk. Firstly, three years earlier, Claude Berri had also adapted Pagnol with two sagas: *Jean de Florette* and *Manon of the Springs*. And secondly, Poiré chose a relatively unknown actor, Philippe Caubère, to play the lead up against Berri's Yves Montand. Difficult but successful: ten million tickets sold for the two films.

Cult films

In 1981, another major presence joined Gaumont. At 37, Patrice Ledoux, a television veteran, initiated a lively and singular style. He produced *Carmen*, just one among a long list of films. For a few months, he headed the circuit. Then he was called upon to replace Toscan du Plantier in 1985 as assistant managing director. He launched *Betty Blue*, the cult film which started the career of actress Béatrice Dalle. Jean-Jacques Beineix's film was soon followed by another cult film: *The Big Blue* by Luc Besson. The box office success—mostly adolescent—was immense even though the critics massacred the film at its premier showing during Cannes 1989. It stayed in French theaters for 171 weeks during which Besson released yet another instant classic: the psychological thriller *Nikita* (1990) for which Anne Parillaud received the César for best actress. Gaumont widened its horizon of auteurs: Bertrand Blier, Michel Blanc, Eric Rochant and even Ridley Scott whose *1492* turned profits in France despite its huge budget.

It was a 1993 comedy film made by Jean-Marie Poiré —Alain's son—which pulverized all recent box office records: *The Visitors*. The film was the most important success of the last 25 years. More than 13 million tickets sold—a fervent audience which would see again and again the picturesque adventures of medieval knight Jean Reno and his servant, Christian Clavier, who get lost in the 20th century.

Fortified by a film library of 5,000 titles of which 500 are sound features and 1,000 hours of newsreels, and an annual production slate of a dozen films—financed for the most part by the company's own fund—Gaumont strides confidently into its second century.

For Jean-Marie Poiré's ninth film, *The Visitors* (produced by Alain Terzian), the director called on Jean Reno and Christian Clavier (center), the team that starred in his previous successful comedy, *Opération Corned Beef*. *Les Visiteurs* recouped its negative costs in less than seven weeks after its release. Below : part of the story board of the film. Next page: Gaumont Grand Ecran Italie, in Paris.

DOCUMENTS

Alice Guy, the woman at Gaumont from the beginning

Starting as a secretary to Léon Gaumont who was then manufacturing cameras, Alice Guy witnessed the discovery of the Cinématographe in December 1895. In the autobiography she wrote while living in the United States , she recalls the emotion shared by all those who witnessed the birth of the 7th Art.

Léon Gaumont received a visit from two old friends : Auguste and Louis Lumière. They had come to invite him to a reception given by the Association for Industrial Development, where the two brothers intended to present a machine they had invented. As I was present at the meeting, they asked me to come along as well, but they refused to tell us anything about their invention.

"You'll see, they said. It's a surprise."

Our curiosity was piqued. We would do our best not to miss the reception.

When we arrived, we saw a white sheet stretched across one of the walls. At the other end of the room, one of the Lumière brothers was manipulating a machine that looked something like a magic lantern.

L*a Première Cigarette* by Alice Guy, 1904.

The lights were dimmed, and on this makeshift screen appeared Lumières' factory. The doors opened, a wave of workers came out, gesticulating, laughing, heading towards restaurants or their homes. Then, one after another, we saw the films which have since become classics: *A Train Arriving in a Station*, *L'Arroseur Arrosé*, etc. We had just witnessed the birth of cinema.

A few days later, the Lumières' Cinematographe gave its first shows in the basement of the Grand Café, 14, Boulevard des Capucines.

There was a great spirit of competition among the inventors. Gaumont, well-advanced in the domain, came in a close second with his chronophotograph. Unfortunately, he thought it wise to use 60 millimeter prints, which necessitated certain transformations and slowed down his start.

But Gaumont, like the Lumière brothers, was especially interested in the mechanics of what he had built. It was just another machine to offer his clients. Shooting film for educational or entertainment purposes didn't seem to attract his attention. However, on the Rue des Sonneries, a small laboratory had been created for developing and printing short subjects: soldiers marching, train stations. Shot by the employees of the laboratory, these short films were used only for demonstrative purposes.

As the daughter of a publisher, I had read a lot and remembered little. I had done some amateur theater and thought it could be done better. Building up my courage, I asked Gaumont if I could write one or two playlets, and to have them acted by friends of mine. Had we known what this idea would develop into, I would never have received his authorization.

Considering my age, my lack of experience, my gender, I had nothing going for me.

But he did give me his permission, as long as none of this impinged upon my secretarial duties. I had to get to the office at 8 a.m., open, register, and distribute the mail. I was then allowed to take the omnibus, drawn by four horses, which climbed the Buttes Chaumont via the Rue La Fayette. I could then make the most of the time allotted to me. At 4:30 p. m. I had to be back at St. Roch to take dictation, get things signed, etc. This often took until 10 or 11 at night. Then, I could at last go home to the Quai Malaquais for a few hours sleep, which I considered well-earned.

Léon Gaumont found that I was wasting too much time with my comings and goings. He offered to fix up a small house he owned at the end of the Rue des Sonneries, behind the photography laboratory, and just a few meters away from the famous platform. (Even so, the rent was 800 francs a year.)

Sensing my hesitation, he promised to install a bathroom and to get a gardener from the Buttes Chaumont to clean up the garden. I ended up giving in. I'd been bitten by the cinema bug. Full of regret, we left our attic room on the Quai Malaquais.

A low wall separated the site from a block of houses belonging to workers of the slaughter houses of La Villette. Not long after we had moved in, horrible shrieks brought me to my window. One of our charming neighbors came home from work to find his wife and daughter on the floor beside a bottle of wine. It was intended for him, and his daughter had dropped it. Wildly angry, he wrapped his unfortunate wife's hair around his wrist. With all his force, he banged her head against the brick wall of their building. I couldn't live with this. Fortunately, the neighbors worried Gaumont too. He ended up heightening the wall; later, he bought the entire block.

This is how I got to know my new surroundings. In the garden, Anatole and I planted our first camera. In 1896, unions didn't exist. People worked 6 days, sometimes 7. There was no limit on how many hours a day. One Sunday morning Gaumont came over and asked me to run laps around the garden, so that he could measure my speed with one of his new inventions. I reiterate : we now call those days "La Belle Epoque".

In Belleville, near the photo laboratory, I was given an unused terrace with an asphalt floor (making it impossible to fix a real set). It was covered with a shaky glass roof and overlooked an empty lot. In this palace, I made my debut as a director. A sheet painted by a neighborhood painter who specialized primarily in scarecrows and the like; a vague set – rows of cabbage constructed by a carpenter; costumes rented around the Porte St. Martin. The cast : my friends, a crying baby, a worried mother. My first film, *La Fée aux Choux* *["The cabbage fairy"]*, thus saw the light. Today it is considered a classic. The Cinémathèque Française has the negative.

I'd be going overboard if I told you it was a masterpiece, but the public wasn't blase and the actors were young and charming. The film was enough of a success that I was allowed to try again.

Thanks to the goodwill of my small staff; thanks to the advice and lessons of Frédéric Dillaye (technical advisor to the Gaumont Corporation and author of excellent books on art photography); thanks to the experience garnered day by day; and thanks to luck and chance – we discovered hundreds of little tricks of the trade. Here are a few of them :

Shooting the film backwards allowed houses being demolished to reconstruct themselves by pure magic; or a person falling from a roof to soar back up spontaneously; or a hungry client in a cake shop, having found the check too pricey, to return the already-eaten pastries intact.

Slowing down or speeding up the crank could turn relaxed pedestrians into frenetic madmen or sleepwalkers.

Stopping the film allowed us to move an object which, during projection, seemed endowed with supernatural powers : an archeologist would thus be stupefied to find his precious mummy playing in the four corners of his laboratory. Example: *The Mummy*.

Shooting from different distances made it possible to place 'in the same frame both pygmies and giants, as in *Lilliput and Gulliver*, *The Ogre and Tom Thumb*, and *The Grandfather Clock's Cakewalk*.

Double exposures.

Dissolves used for visions and

dreams.

We also made some movies on location. During a walk in Barbizon, we came across an old stagecoach. I decided to direct *The Courrier de Lyon*. A theatrical troupe would have been too expensive, so I persuaded my staff to play the parts. Armed with a copious homemade lunch, costumes, props, and a bicycle for almost everyone, we took the train to Melun. At the station, two or three cars, with drivers claiming to be guides of the Fontainebleau forest, took the less athletic young women and the packages. We all set off for Barbizon, where the stagecoach was awaiting us.

The guides took us to a place they considered appropriate. After having savored our picnic, we handed out the costumes. The women did their best behind bushes. The men, less prim, got dressed anywhere. Fortunately, the forest was empty, because we must have been quite a strange sight […].

Despite the brisk autumn weather, our venture was a success. We were full of joy and good humor, and we decided to do it again.

All these short films (of 17 to 25 meters), shot in incredible circumstances, contained the seeds of today's cinema.

In *Total Cinema*, René Barjavel says "Silent films were like a beautiful child playing in the sun, but... when today's youth discovers the cinema from back then, they'll find it somewhat grotesque. They will be surprised at the melancholy of their elders."

[…]

I doubt I'd enjoy seeing my first films. My readers, if I have any, should try to understand the conditions in which we worked : those old, badly adjusted cameras, with their magazines on the outside, the problematic film feeding, the instability of the tripods, used for normal photography, which sank into the earth of our garden. We used only one lens. We wound the film by hand with a crank. The velvet-lined pressure plate attracted dust that scratched the film.

My faithful cameraman Anatole Thiberville (who, before becoming a director, raised chickens in Bresse, if I remember correctly) helped me with undying patience and goodwill. I have excellent memories of him.

The competition that was sprouting up stole our discoveries as soon as we made them. Zecca, the only collaborator who stayed two weeks with me before going to Pathé, made *The Misdeeds of a Calf* (which was later wrongly attributed to me). The film was interesting because it showed the way we could move objects by stopping the camera, as we did in *The Mummy*. Zecca told me that before coming to see me, he sold soap door to door. He would wet the soap to increase its weight. During the screenings at the Rue de Roch, certain clients' reactions were amusing. I remember some who thought it was a trick. They went behind the screen to see whether there were actors miming the scenes.

Alice Guy,
Autobiographie d'une pionnière du cinéma (1873-1968),
Denoël/Gonthier, 1976,
excerpt translated into English
by Andrew Litvack.

The Great War and the First Newsreels

As the First World War is being waged, Louis Feuillade, on the front, is already thinking of his future films. Discharged on July 1915 on account of a bad heart, he began working again and immediately started shooting the series Les Vampires . *As Feuillade was leaving the front, the first newsreel reporters were arriving. A new type of journalism was born. The celebrated reporter Marcel Petiot recounts its beginnings.*

<u>During World War I, Louis Feuillade wrote to his producer, Léon Gaumont, asking for advice concerning cameras</u>

April 28th, 1915

Dear Mr Gaumont,I've received your kind letter of April 26th.

Thank you for the information concerning my captain, but I shall be leaving him shortly for parts unknown -as soon as my transport formation is ready. We're short roughly 30 horses. I suspect we'll have left Lunel by next week. I have to admit life at the depot is depressing, and try as I might I can't manage to drum up much interest in what I'm doing.

Repaving roads will probably be more enjoyable, but as of yet I can't be sure. My fellow-carters are so much more skilled than I that I despair of ever equaling them. I admit, however, that if there had been any chance of selling this military circus abroad, I would have struck a gold mine.

I know Burguet by name. I never heard much about him. There's not much I can tell you about him.

Delighted with the good news about Costil and Garnier. I envy them for seeing action.

As soon as I have an idea for "Bout de Zan", I'll send off a few lines to Mariaud. Until now no inspiration. By 8 pm I can't keep my eyes open, and reveille is at 5 am. There's no counting on finding a corner to think or write. There isn't even a mess in the artillery depot where we're stationed.

I think we should do all we can to

Louis Feuillade, 1919.

keep Perret, but I'm afraid he's going to have to go before another board. There are men here who are much fatter than he and whom they drag into military service...

I hope this letter finds you and your family in good health. Your devoted, affectionate, grateful...

Louis Feuillade

I'd like to take a small camera into the field, with all the necessary equipment. Might I ask your advice concerning the best-suited model?

Léon Gaumont answers Louis Feuillade

May 1st, 1915

My Dear Feuillade,I have received your letter of April 28th.

The Block-Note is the best camera for a soldier, but we're out of stock at the moment. Delivery delays are accumulating, what with 2 workers instead of the usual 50. Nevertheless, I'll keep your request in mind. I'm looking for the kind of set you need at the Studio. Keep me posted on your whereabouts so that we can get the package to you more easily.

I don't believe I'll take B. as a director, even on a trial basis, unless Perret leaves. There's no reason for an absolute refusal, but I'd prefer finding a better solution.

Levesque has just about made a formal demand for his salary. He was soundly ignored by P. I was informed and he's finally going to have to submit his wishes in writing. He wants money, a lot of money!!. I really feel like letting him go. I proposed

terminating or suspending his contract, but he can't come to a decision. He told me during our meeting that he doesn't always think what he writes... so. Public Prosecutor Hallers II... If I find a cameraman, I'll let him do a reel so that he may realize how difficult it is to make a film that can be edited for every country.

Les Deux Français was screened at the Palace Cinema yesterday evening. It was a success, but there were some remarks concerning the subtitle after the victory. We've been obliged to take it off temporarily, in spite of your expressed wishes. It's a good installment in your patriotic series. My compliments once again.

Mariaud is back asking for advances. Where is the poor boy going to wind up? I agree, but I cry bloody murder. He'll be leaving soon for Nice where M. Marechal will keep an eye on him.

Navarre was supposed to be in Marseille today and not only do I hear that he's wandering about Paris, but that he stopped in at P. looking for a job. I found the three toiletry flasks that our friend Coignet delivered late and that were meant for Mademoiselle Isabelle's New Year's gift. It's a little late to send them now, but I'm sending them anyway, hoping you'll forgive me.

I waited in vain for your return from Marseille to give them to you and then... and this is where I am at.

Friendly greetings,
Léon Gaumont

Marcel Petiot : souvenirs of a newsreel reporter

The cinema-gazette, better known as the "newsreel", was created by Pathé in 1907. Less than a year later, Gaumont and Eclair brought out their first newsreels.

From the start, newsreels were a great success with the public, if not with the authorities. Every important event was reported, and moviegoers soon acquired a taste for the reels. Reports were soon being filmed to show the life, customs and events of the most diverse countries.

More akin to journalism than to cinema, newsreels grew by leaps and bounds. The public discovered a reality that even the best written article could not convey. Realizing the importance of this new news medium, other journalists did not immediately accept cinema reporters (or photo reporters for that matter), and many of them took it upon themselves to hamper or disturb the cameramen at work. Since the war, this category of journalists has virtually disappeared, and I must render homage to my colleagues of the written press for the constant support they have been willing to provide newsreel reporters.

As for the authorities, the beginnings were just as difficult. The newsreel reporter with his unwieldy apparatus was universally regarded as an intruder by the authorities. Whether he wanted to enter a government building, an assembly, or a caucus where journalists were welcomed with open arms : impossible, orders were orders, he got no further than the door. The struggle

French President Aristide Briand in the courtyard of the Elysée Palace, 1926.

was arduous until the war, but thanks to the tenacity of the newsreel reporters of the time, events were filmed in the face of any and all opposition, often with makeshift means.

Some anecdotes to illustrate the difficulties : At the Elysée, for example, newsreel reporters were mercilessly sent packing, and it was only thanks to a police superintendant that they were tolerated on the sidewalk across the Faubourg St Honoré. Newsreel reporters gradually became familiar faces and after a while they progressed to the other side of the street. The new position was better, but hardly ideal. The struggle for the next objective lasted longer, and was won only through the intervention of the current Chief Superintendant of the Elysée who argued our case and obtained our authorization to pass through the gates. The situation improved. Times changed and step by step newsreel reporters were allowed to enter the

courtyard, the gardens and even on certain occasions the salons.

When on state journey, newsreel reporters were authorized to enter the president's carriage on the official train, it was considered a victory. Now they are part of the presidential suite and the three specialists of the genre, Krzipow, Martellière and myself, are members of the Association of Presidential Journalists, presided by Jean Rogier of the "Petit Parisien".

When war broke out, the newsreel business, decimated like other businesses, was reorganized with older cameramen, unfit for service. Pathé, Gaumont and Eclair continued with regular newsreels and the public never once missed the week's news. Toward the middle of the war, the government finally understood the impact of cinema and created a Military Photo and Cinema Sector under the command of Captain Pierre Marcel. The sector was made up of some technicians, but mostly of recruits chosen at random from the auxiliary services, and whose aptitudes did not particularly recommend them for this kind of duty. (I've even heard talk of pork butchers.) At the same time, actual reporters, even those already in auxiliary services, were assigned to the most diverse posts. (Such was my case. I was assigned to General Headquarters as a typist, even though I had applied for a transfer to the Cinema Section.)

Cameramen's work in the army was not always facilitated, and I will quote on this subject an excerpt from the book by J. de Pierrefeu, General Headquarters Sector I, concerning the attitude of General Micheler, commander of the Tenth Army : "Hence General Micheler formally forbade the cameraman of the Photo Section to circulate in his sector a few days before they went into action on the Somme. The pictures he took were destined for our propaganda activities in America. General Micheler was guaranteed that the photos would remain under seal until after the attack. He refused to hear of it, and wrote his Superior three times, declining all responsibility for operations, if the reporter continued to take pictures of his army."

Nevertheless, the work of military newsreel reporters, although obscure, was important and often accomplished with great heroism.

Shall I cite Quetin, buried alive with his camera on the front lines of Verdun? Shall I cite all those who at zero hour were out on the parapet with our infantry and stoically filmed the first waves of assault, remaining imperturbable under the rain of bullets. Their heroism, like that of many others, remained obscure, but the result is a collection of filmed war documents that have perhaps never received the care and attention they deserve.

The war ended and the armistice was signed. Unfortunately, the events that took place at the end of 1918 and throughout 1919 were not recorded as they should have been. The Government of the time had a phobia of photography and especially cinema.

Newsreel reporters were driven away and only major outdoor ceremonies could be fairly well filmed. What a pity that the signing of the armistice at Rethondes was not filmed. In a hundred years, the document would have the same value for us as would today a film of Napoleon signing his treaty with the Tsar at Tilsit.

That is unfortunately how things were. How many other events were not recorded as they deserved? The treaty of Versailles, for example, could have been filmed. Although newsreel reporters were admitted, it was only with such difficulty and in such poor conditions that the result was mediocre.

To illustrate the difficulties faced by newsreel reporters during this time, I need only mention the signature of the Treaty of Trianon where photographers and newsreel reporters were flanked by a Service Corps officer whose only concern during the ceremony was to keep the camera tripods in a straight line.

How many times during the peace conference we had to hide in order to steal a shot of Clemenceau! At the time the President detested newsreels. Cameramen had to conspire and take turns sacrificing themselves. One of us would remain conspicuous and without fail the President would turn his back on him, and face the others who had remained hidden. I can remember his appearance at an important meeting at the Quai d'Orsay, during which a journalist managed to stop him thus enabling the cameramen to film him. After several seconds, the President realized he had been ambushed and dismissed the whole lot with a word rendered immortal by Napoleon at Waterloo. Although cinema was silent in those days, lip movements could be read by those in the know.

During the same period, a number of administrative bodies were unequivocally hostile to newsreel reporters, who nevertheless managed to achieve their ends. Certain attempts, however, came within a hair's breadth of catastrophe. During the Grand Prix at Longchamp, Maes flew over the off-limit track to film the event. A badly timed fuel shortage dashed his hopes and forced him to land on the track a few minutes before the starting signal. Maes was greeted by a booing crowd ready to lynch him.

Aviation has always tempted newsreel reporters and I shall only cite for reference the great races filmed by Filippini, Ercole, Dély, etc.

Accidents were no rare occurences, and I need only recall Paul de Klairwal, who almost drowned off Monte Carlo when Roget's hydroplane from which he was shooting a motorboat race suddenly crashed into the sea. Several years later, poor Klairwal was to die at Orly, decapitated by a plane while he and Krzipow were filming an air show. The latter was saved by a quick reflex that cost him only a brush with the airplane, while a few meters away Klairwal was killed as his wife and young daughter watched.

The newsreel reporter touches all domains. Today he may be filming an official ceremony, tomorrow he'll be in the mud or in a driving storm, out at sea or in the midst of military manoeuvres, filming a cataclysm or a revolution. He never knows what tomorrow will bring.

We saw at the beginning of this retrospective that three companies created the newsreel : Pathé, Gaumont and Eclair. Until 1927 nothing changed, the Aubert Journal being only an offshoot of one of these companies.

Until 1927 the newsreels' fortunes varied. They made, but also ate up, a lot of money. Despite the opinion of numerous filmmakers, the public had always loved the news and interest in the news was growing. Many directors and movie theater owners, however, considered the newsreel a fill-in, a curtain raiser, a negligible quantity, and merely a dead weight that cost money. What could be done to diminish the dead weight? Improve it. What did they do? They weighed it down by inserting advertisements. They crippled the newsreel that soon became nothing more than an added bonus, sometimes free, in the featured program. Confronted with diminishing returns, they reduced costs and made the newsreel less interesting, since most of its elements were now no more than disguised publicity. Yet, despite the heavy-handedness, despite the errors, the public remained faithful

to "movie news".

While newsreels were on the decline in France, what was happening abroad? British newsreels were flourishing; four companies were living well on them : Pathé-Gazette, Gaumont-Gazette, Empire News Bulletin, and Topical Budget; a fifth, British Screen News would be created later. In America the news became a prime branch of cinema activity and three companies split the market : Pathé-News, Fox News, and International Newsreel. Three new companies were founded later : Paramount News, MGM News, and Kinograms. The six companies soon opened offices in all the Old World capitals and set up their respective news services in each of these cities.

In brief, while the French newsreels were wasting away, English and American companies, stimulated by their earnings and even more so by professional competition, were growing, and their cameramen were soon omnipresent.

What had to happen happened : in 1927 the Americans grabbed a part of the French market. Pathé and Gaumont merged and under the aegis of Metro-Goldwyn created Pathé Gaumont-Metro News, which appeared weekly and whose only competitor was Eclair-Journal, Aubert and Paramount being only offshoots of Eclair.

Marcel Petiot,
"Memories of a Newsreel Reporter",
Revue du cinéma, 1930,
excerpt translated
by Michael Smith

When the filmgoers protest

A film's opening may give rise to unexpected obstacles. In 1934, Jean Vigo's film Le Chaland qui Passe *("The passing barge") provoked unanimously hostile reactions from theater owners. The audience of the time reacted just as vehemently. Twenty years later,* Un Caprice de Caroline Chérie *was mostly successful because of the steamy reputation of the leading actress, Martine Carol.*

Le Chaland qui passe

In 1934, when, after an already expurgated version of Jean Vigo's Le Chaland qui Passe *(a.k.a.* L'Atalante*) opened, the heated reactions of incensed filmgoers followed quickly.*

September 16 1934

I had never been to the Colisée Theater. The theater itself is pleasing to the eye, the usherettes clean and polite. It is unfortunate, however, that the theater was so unbearably hot.

The film began on time. The first film, *Polar Illusion*, started off well. The pictures are pretty and the sound was good. Unfortunately, there were quite a few slow spots. We were spared no details. We see the Eskimos in their boats ten times, as well as their sleds and their dogs. I appreciated the explanations about the sounding balloons, the old Ford, the sailors dancing with the natives, the white fox. In sum an interesting film in need of quite a few cuts.

On the other hand, the news was too short and not varied enough.

After an intermission, which lasted the normal time, *Le Chaland qui Passe* was shown. Without being either haughty or prejudiced, I can assure you that I've never seen so deplorable a film.

1) The sound is horrid. We don't understand a word of Michel Simon's dialogue, and very little of the others'.

2) The photography is the only good thing in the film. Certain views of the Canal St. Martin are quite lovely.

3) The music : besides the tune of "Le Chaland qui Passe", which is

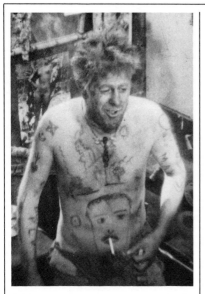

Michel Simon in *L'Atalante*, 1934.

going out of style, the rest of the music wasn't of any interest. I noticed only a few variations of the tune of "Le Chaland qui Passe" which roused our interest.

4) The actors : I wonder what poor Michel Simon is doing in this mess. If his acting hadn't been so appreciated in his earlier films, at the Gymnase and at the Bouffes Parisiens, his future as an actor would indeed be compromised. Dita Parlo is pleasant to watch, as long as she isn't shot in close-ups. They could have done without showing her every two seconds half-naked. Jean Dasté is lousy. Why does he take various unaesthetic nude poses? The peddler in the dance hall should learn to speak French without an accent.

5) The story could have been written by a five year-old, if we ignore the sexual issues. There's nothing to remember. Michel Simon's tatoos are in rather bad taste, as is the scene in which Jean Dasté wriggles about in his bed while Dita Parlo does the same in hers.

To close, I think that such a film is harmful to cinema in general. If money wasn't at stake, there would be good reason to remove it from the theaters. The public would share my opinion. Throughout the film, I heard whistling, gibes, and ironic applause, to such an extent that the projection was almost cut short. I heard no favorable reactions, and quite a few people left the theater before the film ended.

Georges Lazard

September 19 1934

Monsieur,
In my capacity as a former Secretary General of the Palais Royal theater, I observed with great sadness, after the projection of *Le Chaland qui Passe* at the Colisée, the mediocrity, the "couldn't-give-a-damn" attitude, and the unbelievable bad taste of those who contributed to the editing of this film. I don't think they can be French; their licenses should be taken away for the sake of the filmgoers and of silent cinema (sic) in general.

Monsieur Berlioz

Caroline Chérie's whims

Long after the scandal surrounding Jean Vigo's film, Caroline Chérie's *indiscretions provoked reactions from both filmgoers and theater owners.*

Monsieur,
Following the telephone calls between the management of the Berry and your service, and the report submitted to your Bordeaux office by Monsieur Deschamps, we are obliged to recount to you the unfortunate incidents surrounding *Caroline Chérie*.

These daily incidents have had serious consequences which threaten to grow worse. They are the work of the clergy and various Catholic groups in Poitiers.

During Sunday mass on both the 22th and the 29th of March, priests in certain churches have incited their congregations to "write to the theater managers, demanding the cancellation of this licentious film". We have received several letters : some of them are anonymous, others contain threats.

Indeed, during the past week, despite police surveillance, distasteful remarks have been written with oil-based paint on the window and walls of the theater. The damage totals several thousand francs.

Yesterday, two seats were ripped open with a knife. Certain shop-owners who agreed to display posters of the film in their shops have been insulted in public by their outraged clients.

Yesterday the Mayor suggested by telephone that we stop advertizing the film entirely.

These incidents are justified in the following way : with this film, our box office has been pulling in 10,000 to 12,000 francs a day.

Despite our goodwill, you will understand that it is materially impossible to continue showing this film much longer, especially during Holy Week. This decision has been made to preserve the prestige of your company and the reputation of our theater.

We thus will stop showing *Caroline Chérie* this evening.

The Manager
The Berry Theater
Poitiers, March 31 1953

Banning of the projection of «Caroline Chérie».

Public censorship was paralleled by legal censorship.

We, the Mayor of Niort;
In view of the decree of May 7, 1936, concerning cinematographic ruling, and especially Article 10 of the aforementioned decree;

Graffiti covering the front of a movie theater playing *Un Caprice de Caroline chérie*, 1953.

In view of Article 97 of the Law of April 5, 1884;

Whereas the film entitled *Caroline Chérie*, directed by Cécil Saint-Laurent was supposed to show in two theaters in our city : the Cinema Eden, rue de la Comédie, and the Cinema Rex, Avenue de la République, from June 2 to June 7;

Whereas the projection of this film has provoked certain incidents in other cities;

Whereas the projections planned in Niort have raised in advance many vehement demonstrations on the behalf of different people and organizations, especially the Family Movement;

Whereas, after our intervention, the Eden Cinema has refused to show the aforementioned film;

Whereas, despite our intervention, both oral and written, and despite the pressure from citizens and organizations, the management of the Rex Cinema seems to persist in its intention to show the film;

Whereas, having taken note of the opinions of many of our administrators, it is feared that public order will be disrupted in our city if this film is shown; and that, in order to avoid this trouble – in the interest of the management of the Rex Cinema;

It is decreed :

Article One : All projections of *Caroline Chérie* are hereby forbidden in Niort theaters.

Article Two : The Police Commissioner is charged to execute this decree. Monsieur Lafarge, manager of the Rex Cinema, shall be notified accordingly.

City Hall. Niort. May 30 1953

The Mayor
F. Lélant

Excerpts translated by Andrew Litvack.

Producing today

The relations between directors and producers are quite often delicate, as witnessed by the story of Nicolas Seydoux's visit to the set of The Big Blue, *and by an exchange of letters between Patrice Ledoux and Francesco Rosi concerning the opera-film* Carmen.

<u>**Producer Nicolas Seydoux payed a visit to the crew of «The Big Blue».**</u>

September 29th. Nicolas Seydoux, the man who gave the green light to a 75-million franc budget, arrives in a helicopter. Perfect timing : after the enormous amount of energy expended and the miracles brought about during the storm, now we're shooting a bargain-basement scene in a bizarre atmosphere : Mayol's dream of Johana dancing in the middle of the sky.

Miss Arquette is placed on top of a cube. Luc sets up a low-angle shot. He chooses a very slow speed. We wait for the sun to peek through the clouds.

"Now! Go ahead! Dance!"

Rosanna remains motionless on her cube, her arms hanging down, her

The crew of *The Big Blue.*

bangs covering her eyes and her mouth all twisted.

"What should I dance? Tell me."

"It doesn't matter."

She pauses for a second, then starts doing an irresistible belly-dance. Luc is hysterical laughing.

"Something more modern! Move your arms!"

Rosanna crosses her arms and broods.

"I need music."

An assistant goes off to look for a tape deck. He comes back five minutes later, but the cord is too short to plug it in on the terrace. His arms behind his back, eschewing any commentary, Nicolas Seydoux watches this scene perfectly calm. The assistant becomes beet red.

"An extension cord, dammit!"

Rosanna is tapping her foot on the cube. The sun hides behind a cloud. At that point, Marc Duret comes forward, trying to keep his head high. "Well, if that's the way it is, I'll sing."

Jean Reno tries to stop him : "Don't do that!"

"Yes, if it is necessary... I will sacrifice myself." And Marc breaks into a very personal rendition of *Strangers in the Night*, heavily influenced by Julio Iglesias. Rosanna wrinkles her brow, shrugs her shoulders and starts dancing.

Luc shouts "Action!".

Hearing this brouhaha, the cook comes out onto the terrace. Wide-eyed, he stares at Rosanna, Marc and Luc. The wrinkles on his forehead show us how troubled he is.

"Is this for real? This is going to be in the movie?"

At 11 p.m., we start shooting again.

This time, we shoot the scene where Johana discovers Jacques after his nightmare. His ears and eyes are covered with blood. His bedroom windows are all shattered. Luc explains to Rosanna that she must scream when she sees him in this sorry state. There's just a small crew in the bungalow; the others are waiting outside. Suddenly, a shriek tears through the night, followed immediately by a loud guffaw Rosanna explodes. "I can't do this! This isn't a horror movie." Luc shrugs his shoulders: "It's a normal reaction."

"No!"

"Yes!"

"No, it's tacky."

Luc takes a deep breath. "Yes, it's tacky. It's what I want... De Niro would be tacky too in a similar situation. The truth of this scene is not that you're intelligent, but that you're confused, panic-stricken. You're afraid, and fear is tacky. You're not pretty!"

Rosanna lifts her hand in front of her mouth, pensive.

One hour later, she's sipping a cocktail through a straw, her elbows on the bar, her legs wrapped around the stool.

"The main thing about Luc's work is that he's mostly interested in the camera. I need to be stimulated permanently, so I annoy him, I provoke him. I don't want to adapt myself to him, I want him to adapt himself to my needs. In the United States, an actor is much more respected and protected than he is here. He is spared most of the annoying aspects of the shoot. This is necessary so he or she can give

Toscan du Plantier, P. Ledoux and N. Seydoux during the shooting of *Carmen*.

his utmost. Like many American actors, I'm a professional, obsessed by details. I want things to seem credible. I know what I want!

Le Grand Bleu, Ramsay, 1988

Close negotiations concerning the budget of film «Carmen».

When a film costs more than expected, it is the producer's role to argue the case to the director. Below, Patrice Ledoux addresses Francesco Rosi

Paris, September 2, 1983
Dear Francesco,
The various difficulties we have encountered during the shoot have forced us to lengthen the filming schedule and especially to use all the contingency.

In order to remain within budget, and according to President Seydoux's instructions, which were confirmed by Daniel Toscan du Plantier during his last visit to Carmona, I am obliged to ask you to cut out certain scenes from the script.

I am referring in particular to what you wished to film in Cordoba.

I want you to know that I understand and share your artistic concerns. The Guadalquivir, a certain urban connotation, will be missing from the film, and its editing will surely be more difficult. However, despite all your preoccupations, you did agree to take into consideration the economic constraints to which I must hold myself. I am thus assuming full responsibility for this decision, and I thank you for the understanding you showed me earlier.

One last word, and I ask you to take it not as flattery, but as recognition of your talent and your character : I know that in spite of this you will find the solutions necessary to make this film resemble you, as does every project you undertake.

Patrice.

Carmona, September 3, 1983
Dear Patrice,
The "lengthening of the filming schedule" you mentioned has been, as you know and as is easy to prove, caused by things that don't concern me. They concern me no more than the depletion of the contingency. (I can only regret that the amount put aside didn't permit me to cover those unexpected whims, as well as those I shall refer to in this little "love letter".) That is why I cannot accept your reasons for justifying the cuts you want me to make. But at the stage we're at, I can only adapt to the decisions of my producers. However, let me note that, as you are aware, these cuts will be, in one way or another, felt in the general context of the narrative. At the same time, let me reassure you that I shall continue working in this spirit of cooperation which I do thank you for recognizing.
Sincerely,

Francesco Rosi.

Paris, March 1984
President Seydoux, my dear friend, I saw *Carmen* at the Paris Cinema. This film is marvelous. If, because of its cost, it brings in no profits; even if it results in losses – all this is of no importance, because from time to time, we must think of art.
Sincerely,
Marcel Dassault

excerpts translated by
Andrew Litvack

Francesco Rosi directing *Carmen*.

Gaumont theater circuit

Gaumont is constantly reorganizing its theater circuit. At present, in 1994, the company disposes of a conglomeration of theaters covering all of France, and is leader in Paris. In this way, Gaumont is continuing its policy of integrating film production into the domain of distribution, the purpose of which is above all to reach the largest public possible.

Gaumont in Paris
18 theaters, 73 screens

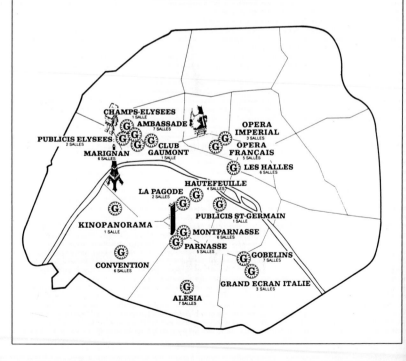

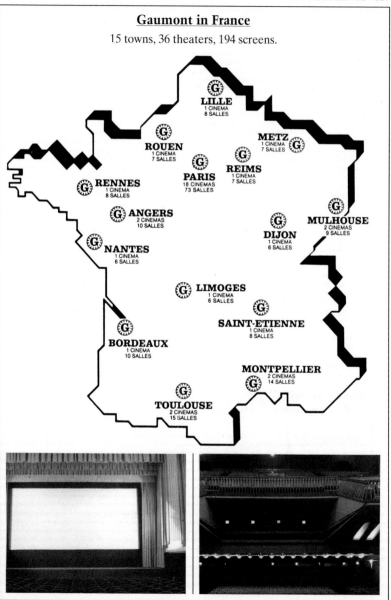

Gaumont in France

15 towns, 36 theaters, 194 screens.

LILLE
1 CINEMA
8 SALLES

METZ
1 CINEMA
7 SALLES

ROUEN
1 CINEMA
7 SALLES

PARIS
18 CINEMAS
73 SALLES

REIMS
1 CINEMA
7 SALLES

RENNES
1 CINEMA
8 SALLES

ANGERS
2 CINEMAS
10 SALLES

MULHOUSE
2 CINEMAS
9 SALLES

DIJON
1 CINEMA
6 SALLES

NANTES
1 CINEMA
6 SALLES

LIMOGES
1 CINEMA
6 SALLES

SAINT-ETIENNE
1 CINEMA
8 SALLES

BORDEAUX
1 CINEMA
10 SALLES

MONTPELLIER
2 CINEMAS
14 SALLES

TOULOUSE
2 CINEMAS
15 SALLES

CHRONOLOGY

1864 Birth of Léon Gaumont
1881 Léon Gaumont is hired as a secretary by Carpentier
1888 Léon Gaumont marries Camille Maillard
1893 Léon becomes head of the Comptoir Général de la Photographie
1894 Georges Demeny is hired by Gaumont
1895 The Comptoir Général de la Photographie becomes Société Léon Gaumont & cie, with a capital of 200 000 F.
1896 The Demeny Chrono, first Gaumont projector, is built
1897 The Demeny Chronophotographe. Alice Guy directs her first Gaumont films
1903 Presentation of the Chronophone, a combination of cinema and the phonograph
1905 Creation of the Théâtre Cinématographique Gaumont at the Buttes Chaumont
1906 Creation of the Société des Etablissements Gaumont (SEG), capital 2 500 000 F, presided by Pierre Azaria
1907 Emile Cohl makes the first cartoon. Louis Feuillade enters Gaumont. Capital raised to 3 000 000 F
1908 Creation of Gaumont Ltd in London
1910 Creation of the Comptoir Ciné-Location, directed by E. Costil. Léon Gaumont presents the Chronophone at the Académie des Sciences. The Hippodrome de la Place Clichy is bought
1911 The Hippodrome de Clichy becomes the Gaumont Palace
1912 Creation of Gaumont Cie, with a capital of 500 000 US$. Presentation of the Gaumont Chronochrome, which announces color films
1913 Capital raised to 4 000 000 F. Opening of the studios in Nice. Feuillade directs the first Gaumont serials, *Fantômas*
1919 Capital 5 000 000 F
1921 Capital 10 000 000 F
1922 Creation of GEG Gaumont Films, presided by Léon Gaumont
1924 Sale of the Gaumont subsidiary in London to Broomhead
1925 Death of Feuillade. Production stops, except the Feuillade production, taken over by his son-in-law. Launching of Gaumont Metro Goldwyn. Agreement with Electrical Fono Films, a Danish society, to improve sound
1927 Capital 12 000 000 F. Public presentation of the Filmphone. Launching of *Pathé Gaumont Métro Actualités*
1928 Presentation of the Gaumont Elgéphone.

Gaumont and Metro Goldwyn split
1929 Capital raised to 24 000 000 F, thanks to the BNC. Presentation of the Idéal Sonore. Léon Gaumont gives up the direction of the society
1930 Capital raised to 84 000 000 F. The Vice-President of the BNC becomes President of SEG. Creation of GFFA. Renting of the St Maurice studios to Paramount
1931 Capital raised to 100 000 000 F
1932 Léon Gaumont resigns. Paul Keim becomes general manager of GFFA. Launching of *France Actualités Gaumont*, headed by Germaine Dulac
1935 General Targe takes over from Paul Keim as President. Bankrupcy of Pathé. GFFA goes into liquidation
1936 Capital reduced to 5 000 000 F. Strikes in the Gaumont studios
1938 General Targe resigns. Havas takes control of GFFA. Birth of the Société Nouvelle des Etablissements Gaumont (SNEG) presided by Léon Rénier; capital 12 975 000 F. Alain Poiré hired by SNEG
1940 Capital raised to 19 500 000 F
1941 The Compagnie des Compteurs takes control of SNEG. Gaumont buys out the Société des Films Marcel Pagnol. Creation of a production departement
1942 SNEG subscribes to the capital of *France Actualités*
1945 Agreement with Rank, creation of Gaumont-Eagle-Lion
1946 Capital raised to 121 500 000 F. Death of Léon Gaumont
1947 Creation of the Société Générale de Travaux Cinématographiques
1948 *Gaumont Actualités* absorbs Metro Journal
1952 First Technicolor film coproduced with Cinéphonic
1953 Inauguration of the stereo system and large screens (22 x 13,5m) at the Gaumont Palace
1954 Transfer of the Nice and Riviera studios
1956 Capital raised to 607 500 000 F
1958 Deregulation of movie ticket prices
1960 SNEG takes share in a company studying pay-TV. Showing of the Rome Olympics, in association with ORTF and Philips at the Bosquet Gaumont
1961 Capital raised to 12 150 000 NF. SNEG relaunches shorts and educational films. Agreement between Gaumont and Metro Goldwyn Mayer. Creation of Gaumont International
1962 Capital raised to 18 225 000 F
1963 The Gaumont Palace is turned into Cinérama

1964 Creation of Gaumont Italiana
1966 Theater programming accord Gaumont/Pathé
1967 Electronique Marcel Dassault equips the Gaumont circuit for TV broadcasting
1968 10 000 televisions across France
1969 *Gaumont Actualités* absorbs *Actualités Eclair*
1970 Agreement with Télécip to produce and distribute TV programs. Three new administrators: J.-Pierre de Launoit, Paul Lepercq, Jérôme Seydoux
1971 First multiplexes
1972 GIE Gaumont Pathé. Closing-up of the Gaumont Palace
1974 The Compagnie des Compteurs no longer controls Gaumont. Jérôme Seydoux is no longer administrator in Gaumont
1975 Nicolas Seydoux becomes chairman and chief executive officer. Daniel Toscan du Plantier, assistant managing director. Opening of the Evry multiplex. Launching of Document de la Semaine, replacing *Gaumont Actualités*
1977 Distribution agreement with 20th Century Fox
1978 Creation of Gaumont do Brazil, Gaumont Italia and Gaumont Inc.; launching of Téléfrance with Sofirad
1979 *Don Giovani* is the first of a series of opera-films. Launching of Gaumont Musique
1980 Creation of Gaumont Editions Musicales, purchasing of Editions Costallat-record Erato. End of *Gaumont Actualités*. Beginning of the coproductions with Marcel Dassault
1981 Purchasing of publishing house Ramsay
1982 Purchasing of weekly news magazine *Le Point*. Creation of Edivisuel with publishing house Gallimard. End of the agreement with 20th Fox
1983 Liquidation of Téléfrance, of the Italian activities, of the Ramsay publishing house. Liquidation of the GIE Pathé Gaumont
1984 End of Gaumont do Brazil. Nicolas Seydoux takes 10,5% of the capital
1985 Transfer of *Le Point* to Cinépar, transfer of Erato. Daniel Toscan du Plantier leaves the company. Launching of the Gaumontrama theaters. Gaumont partner at 25% of TV6 with Publicis
1989 Transfer of Ramsay to publisher Desforges. Launching of a new TV channel with CGE
1990 Launching of Gaumont Robur TV. Capital raised to 232 000 000 F. Jérôme Seydoux buys out Pathé
1991 Distribution agreement with Disney. Gaumont buys out Robur's share. Launching of Gaumont Télévision. Acquisition of the Kinopanorama theater

FURTHER READING

– R. Binet, *Les Sociétés de Cinématographe*, Etudes financières, Paris, 1908
– M. Coissac, *Histoire du Cinématographe*, Editions du «Cinéopse»/Gauthier-Villars, Paris, 1925
– Jacques Deslandes, *Histoire Comparée du Cinéma*, 2 volumes, Casterman, Tournai, 1966
– Henri Fescourt, *Le Cinéma, des Origines à nos Jours*, Editions du Cygne, Paris, 1932
– Louis Gaumont, *Léon Gaumont et ses Collaborateurs..... du Cinéma et bien d'Autres Choses*, manuscript, 2 volumes
– Alice Guy, *Autobiographie d'une Pionnière du Cinéma 1873/1968*, Denoël/Gonhier, Paris, 1976
– Ph. d'Hugues & D. Muller, *Gaumont 90 ans de Cinéma*, Ramsay/Cinémathèque Française, Paris, 1986
– Alain Poiré, *200 Films au Soleil*, Ramsay, Paris, 1988
– Léon Poirier, *24 Images à la Seconde, Journal d'un Cinéaste*, Mame, Paris, 1953
– Georges Sadoul, *Histoire Générale du Cinéma*, 6 volumes, Denoël, Paris 1954
– Alan Williams, *Republic of Images, A History of French Filmmaking*, Londres, 1992
– Annual report of GFFA, 1931 to 1934
– Annual report of SEG, then Société Gaumont, 1940 to 1992.
– Gaumont Newsreels, 1910 to 1980

LIST OF ILLUSTRATIONS

Key: **a**=above; **b**=below; **l**=left; **r**=right; **c**=center.
Front cover. Left (from top to bottom): *Les Vampires*, L. Feuillade (1916); *La Passion de Jeanne d'Arc*, C. Dreyer (1928); *La Poison*, S. Guitry (1951); *La Chèvre*, F. Veber (1981); *The Big Blue*, L. Besson (1988); *My Father's Glory*, Y. Robert (1990); *The Visitors*, J.M. Poiré (1993). Right: *Fantômas* (1923). **Back cover** Poster advertising the Gaumont Chronophone . **Spine** A Gaumont logo. *1* Poster advertising the Gaumont Chronophone (circa 1915). *2* Poster advertising a documentary distributed by Gaumont (1923). *3* Poster advertising Gaumont documentaries (1917-25). *4* Poster for *Le Retour du Croisé* by Louis Feuillade (1908). *5* Poster for *Scaramouche* by Rex Ingram, distributed by Gaumont (1923). *6* Poster for *Le Stigmate* by Feuillade (1924). *7* Poster for *Bouboule 1er Roi Nègre* by Léon Mathot (1933). *10* Cover of the *Bulletin Cinématographique Mensuel* (June 1926). *11* Léon Gaumont in his artillery uniform (1890). *12* Poster advertising the Gaumont company

(circa. 1900).

12/13 Léon Gaumont presents the Demeny Chronophotographe (circa 1900).

13 First Gaumont logo.

14 The Gaumont Chronophone-Mégaphone.

15a Carnival house used as a movie house.

15b Gaumont workshops (1920's).

16 (from top to bottom) *La Fée aux Choux* (1900), *Le Testament de Pierrot* (1904), *L'Electrocutée* (1904), films by Alice Guy.

16br Alice Guy in 1895.

17 Shooting of *Mignon*, a comic opera by A. Thomas (1906).

18a *Deauville*, a film shot in the Trichrome process (1913), Kodak foundation, Rochester, USA.

18b Staff of the Comptoir Ciné-Location (1920's).

19 The Gaumont Palace in 1918.

20a Program for the Gaumont Palace, 1913.

20b/21a Advertisements for the following films: *Bout de Zan Vole un Eléphant* by Feuillade (1915) and *Triste Aventure d'Onésime* by Jean Durand (1913).

21b Advertisement for the "Ben Hur perfume", published in a Gaumont Palace program (1927).

21br Renée Carl (1920's).

22 *Onésime Débute au Théâtre* by Jean Durand (1913).

22br Louis Feuillade (circa 1900).

23a Advertisement for *Cent Dollars Mort ou Vif* by Jean Durand (1912).

23b Drawing in a publicity brochure

for the *Gaumont Actualités* (1920's)

24 *Bébé Adopte un Petit Frère* by Feuillade (1912).

25a Poster for *Fantômas* by Feuillade (1915).

25b Berthe Dagmar in *Le Collier Vivant* by Jean Durand (1913).

26 Printing advertising material in the Gaumont printshop (circa 1925).

26/27b Aerial view of Cité Elgé (circa 1910).

27a American newsreel reporters in 1917, *Gaumont Actualités*.

28 Poster for *Judex* by Louis Feuillade (1917).

29b *Une Page de Gloire*, by Léonce Perret (1915).

29r Aerial camera built to be mounted on the Goliath bomber, 1918.

30a (from left to right) *Narayana* (Poirier, 1920), *L'Orpheline* (Feuillade, 1921), *Le Fils du Flibustier* (Feuillade, 1922).

30b Poster for *Douglas Reporter* by Joseph Henabery, distributed by Gaumont (1918).

31b Detail taken from a poster advertising *Barabbas* by Louis Feuillade (1919).

32a *Le Pied qui Etreint* by J. Feyder (1916).

32b Portrait of René Clair in *Parisette* by Louis Feuillade (1922).

33a Poster for *L'Epreuve du Feu,*a Victor Sjöström film distributed by Gaumont (1921).

33 Léon Gaumont and Charles Pathé (1930's).

34 Poster for *La Tentatrice*, a Fred Niblo film distributed by Gaumont (1927).

34-35 Drawing taken from a poster celebrating

the agreement between SEG and Metro-Goldwin (1925).

35 Ramon Novarro in *Ben Hur* by Fred Niblo (1927).

36 Dita Parlo in *Le Chaland qui Passe* by Jean Vigo (1934).

37 The "Ideal-sonore" projector (1929).

38 *Roumanie, Terre d'Amour* by Camille de Morlhon (1930).

39l Advertisement for Aubert film company.

39d (from top to bottom) Logos of the following companies : Aubert, Franco-Film, Aubert-Franco-Film, GFFA.

40h Laurence Clavius in *Daïnah la Métisse* by Jean Grémillon (1931).

40b Poster for *La Tragédie de la Mine* by G. W. Pabst (1931).

41 The Gambetta theater in Paris (1920').

42 Refurbishment of the Gaumont Palace (1931).

43a Power generator in the underground of the Gaumont Palace, 1931.

43b Organ of the Gaumont Palace, 1931.

44c Georges Milton in *Bouboule Ier, Roi Nègre* by Léon Mathot (1933).

44b Paul Keim and George Milton.

45 *La Mille et Deuxième Nuit* by Alexandre Volkoff (1933).

46 Publicity material for *Le Miracle des Loups* by R. Bernard (1924).

47a Poster by René Peron for *Le Chaland qui Passe (L'Atalante)* by Jean Vigo, 1934.

47b Jean Vigo and Dita Parlo during the shooting of *Le Chaland qui Passe* by Jean Vigo,

1934.

48 Portrait of Germaine Dulac (1920's).

49a Advertisement for *Gaumont Actualités*.

49b Strikes during the Popular Front.

50 Publicity material for *Sahara*, a documentary by Joseph Faivre, 1930.

51 Marcel Petiot's press card, may 1938.

52 Entrance of the Royal theater in Lyon during *Les Rendez-vous deJuillet* by Jacques Becker (1949).

53 Food card during the German Occupation.

54 Poster by Roger Cartier for *Le Journal Tombe à 5 Heures* by Georges Lacombe (1942).

54/55 The Marignan theater during the German Occupation.

55 Card authorizing Alain Poiré to produce (1942), coll. A. Poiré.

56 Poster by Roger Vacher for *Les Cadets de l'Océan* by Jean Dréville (1942).

56/57 Michèle Alfa in *Jeannou* by Léon Poirier (1943).

57 Georges Marchal and Michel Simon in *Vautrin*, by Pierre Billon (1943).

58 Poster by Jean-Denis Malclès for *La Belle et la Bête* by Jean Cocteau (1945).

59a Poster by Dubout for *Le Dictateur* by Charlie Chaplin (1945).

59b Noël-Noël in *La Cage aux Rossignols* de Jean Dréville (1944).

60 Poster by Jacques Bonneaud for *Les Démons de l'Aube* by Yves Allégret (1945).

60/61 Roger Pigaut and Claire Mafféi in *Antoine*

INDEX OF FILMS PRODUCED OR DISTRIDUTED BY GAUMONT

Televisione Italiana, Vides Produzione SRL, Gaumont, Films A2. Dir.: Federico Fellini. Starring: Freddie Jones, Barbara Jefford. P. 81, *86*.

Antoine et Antoinette, 1947. Prod.: SNEG. Dir.: Jacques Becker. Starring: Claire Maffei, Roger Pigaut, Annette Poivre. P. 61, *61*, 62.

Arizona Bill (series) 1909. Prod.: Gaumont. Dir.: Jean Durand. Starring: Joe Hamman. P. 24.

As des As (L'), 1982. Prod.: Gaumont. Dir.: Gérard Oury. Starring: Jean-Paul Belmondo, Marie-France Pisier. P. *90*.

Astérix et la Surprise de César, 1985. Prod.: Gaumont, Dargaud, productions René Goscinny. Dir.: Paul and Gaëtan Brizzi. P *89*.

Atalante (L'), 1934. Prod.: Jacques Louis-Nounez. Dir.: Jean Vigo. Starring: Dita Parlo, Fanny Clair, Jean Dasté, Michel Simon. P. *47*, 108, 109.

Au Pays des Basques (documentary), 1930. Prod.: GFFA. Dir.: Maurice Champreux. P. *50*.

Bande à Bouboule (La), 1931. Prod.: GFFA. Dir.: Léon Mathot. Starring: Mona Goya, Lily Zévaco, Georges Milton, Louis Kerly. P. *44*.

Barbouzes (Les), 1964. Prod.: Gaumont. Dir.: Georges Lautner. Starring: Mireille Darc, Lino Ventura, Bernard Blier, Francis Blanche. P. *72*, 73.

Barrabas, 1919. Prod.: Gaumont. Dir.: Louis Feuillade. Starring: Blanche Montel, Gaston Michel, Violette Jyl. P *31*.

Beauty and the Beast, 1946. Prod.: SNEG, André Paulvet. Dir.: Jean Cocteau. Starring: Josette Day, Jean Marais, Michel Auclair. P. *58*, 59.

Bébé Adopte un Petit Frère, 1912. Prod.: Gaumont. Dir.: Louis Feuillade. Starring: Renée Carl, Clément Mary, René Poyen. P. *24*.

Belles de Nuit (Les), 1952. Prod.: Franco London Films, Rizzoli Films. Dir.: René Clair. Starring: Gina Lollobrigida, Martine Carol, Gérard Philipe. P. *32*.

Ben Hur, 1926. Prod.: MGM. Distr.: Gaumont Metro Goldwin. Dir.: Charles Brabin and Fred Niblo. Starring: Ramon Novarro, Francis Bushman, Carmel Myers. P. 32, *35*.

Betty Blue, 1986. Prod.: Claudie Ossard, Jean-Jacques Beineix. Dir.: Jean-Jacques Beineix. Starring: Béatrice Dalle, Jean-Hugues Anglade, Gérard Darmon, Clémentine Célarié. P. *77*, 94.

Big Blue (The), 1988. Prod.: Gaumont. Dir.: Luc Besson. Starring: Rosanna Arquette, Jean-Marc Barr, Jean Reno. P. *77*, *92*, 94.

Big Parade (The), 1927. Prod.: Metro Goldwyn. Distr. : GMG. Dir.: King Vidor. Starring: Claire Adams, John Gilbert, Karl Dane. P. 34.

Bouboule, 1ᵉʳ Roi Nègre, 1933. Prod.: GFFA. Dir.: Léon Mathot. Starring: Georges Milton, Simone Deguyse, Victor Vina. P. *44*.

Boulogne-sur-Mer (documentary), 1897. Prod.: Gaumont (CGC). P. 13.

Boum (La), 1980 & *Boum 2 (La)*, 1982. Prod.: Gaumont International, Sté de Production des Films Marcel-Dassault. Dir.: Claude Pinoteau. Starring: Claude Brasseur, Brigitte Fossey, Sophie Marceau. P. 92, *92*.

Cadets de l'Océan (Les), 1945. Prod.: SNEG, Centre des Jeunes du Cinéma. Réal.: Jean Dréville. Starring: Blanchette Brunoy, Jean Paqui, Marcel Mouloudji. P. 56.

Cage aux Rossignols (La), 1945. Prod.: SNEG. Dir.: Jean Dréville. Starring: Micheline Francey, Noël-Noël, René Blancard. P. *59*, 61.

Caprice de Caroline Chérie (Un), 1953. Prod.: SNEG, Cinéphonic. Dir.: Jean Devaivre. Starring: Martine Carol, J. Dacqmine, J. Dufilho. P. 62, *62*.

Carmen, 1984. Prod.: Gaumont. Dir.: Francesco Rosi. Starring: Julia Migenes-Johnson, Placido Domingo. P. 80, *83*, 94.

Caroline Chérie, 1951. Prod.: SNEG, Cinéphonic. Dir.: Richard Pottier. Starring: .Martine Carol, Marie Déa, Jacques Dacqmine. P. 62, 109, 110, 111.

Casse-pieds (Les), 1948. Prod.: SNEG, Cinéphonic. Dir.: Jean Dréville. Starring: Marguerite Deval, Noël-Noël, Bernard Blier, Henri Crémieux. P. 62.

Cent Dollars Mort ou Vif, 1912. Prod.: Gaumont. Dir.: Jean Durand. Starring: Berthe Dagmar, Joe Hamman, Gaston Modot. P. *23*.

Cent Mille Dollars au Soleil, 1964. Prod.: Gaumont International. Dir.: .Henri Verneuil. Starring: J.-P. Belmondo, Lino Ventura, Bernard Blier. P. *72*, 73.

Cerveau (Le), 1969. Prod.: Gaumont International. Dir.: Gérard Oury. Starring: Sophie Grimaldi, Jean-Paul Belmondo, Bourvil, David Niven. P. 74, 75.

Chaland qui Passe (Le), see *L'Atalante*.

Chèvre (La), 1981. Prod.: Gaumont International, Fideline Films. Dir.: Francis Veber. Starring: Pierre Richard, Gérard Depardieu. P. *88*, 92.

Chine Eternelle (documentary), après 1929. Prod.: L. Wechsler. Distr. : GFFA. P. *50*.

City of Women, 1980. Prod.: Gaumont, Opera Films. Dir.: Federico Fellini. Starring: Anna Prucnal, Marcello Mastroiani, Ettore Manni. P. 81.

Collier de la Reine (Le), 1929. Prod.: GFFA. Dir.: Gaston Ravel, Tony Lekain. Starring: Jean Weber, Marcelle Jefferson-Cohn. P. 45.

Comte de Monte Cristo (Le), 1961. Prod.: Films Jean-Jacques Vital, Films René Modiano, SNEG, Cinériz Royal Film. Dir.: Claude Autant-Lara. Starring: Yvonne Furneaux, Louis Jourdan, Pierre Mondy, Henri Guisol. P. *69*.

Condamné à Mort s'est Echappé (Un), 1956. Prod.: SNEG, Nouvelles Editions de Films. Dir.: Robert

Daniel Vigne. P. 89.

Invité du Mardi (L'), 1950. Prod.: SNEG, Films Raoul Ploquin. Dir.: Jacques Deval. Starring: M. Robinson, Bernard Blier, Michel Auclair. P. 62.

Je Vous Salue Marie, 1985. Prod.: Pégase, JLG, Sara Films, SSR, Channel 4, Distr: Luna Gerick, Gaumont France. Dir.: Jean-Luc Godard. Starring: Myriem Roussel, Juliette Binoche. P. 85.

Jeannou, 1943. Prod.: SNEG. Dir.: Léon Poirier. Starring: Michèle Alfa, Roger Duchesnes, Saturnin Fabre. P. 57, *57*.

Journal Tombe à 5 Heures (Le), 1942. Prod.: SNEG. Dir.: Georges Lacombe. Starring: Bernard Blier, Marie Déa, Pierre Fresnay, P. Renoir. P. 54, 55, *55*.

Judex, 1917. Prod.: Gaumont. Dir.: .Louis Feuillade. Starring: Musidora, Yvette Andreyor. P *28*, 29.

Lanciers Noirs (Les), 1962. Prod.: SNEG, Royal Film. Distr.: Gaumont. Réal. : Giacomo Gentilomo. Starring: Mel Ferrer, Yvonne Furneaux. P. 89.

Léonce, 1913-1915. Prod.: Gaumont. Dir.: Léonce Perret. Starring: Léonce Perret, Suzanne Le Bret , Suzanne Grandais. P. 25.

Loulou, 1980. Prod.: Action Films, Gaumont. Dir.: Maurice Pialat. Starring: Isabelle Huppert, Gérard Depardieu. P. *80*.

Lucky Luke, les Dalton en Cavale, 1983. Prod.: Gaumont, FR3, Hanna-Barbera and Dargaud Editeur. Dir.: Morris et Bil Hanna. P. *85*.

Mais où Est donc Passé la 7e Compagnie?, 1973. Prod.: SNEG, Euro International Film. Dir.: Robert Lamoureux. Starring: Jean Lefebvre, Pierre Mondy, Aldio Maccione, Robert Lamoureux. P. 75.

Marche à l'Ombre, 1984. Prod.: Christian Fechner, Films A2. Dir.: Michel Blanc. Starring: Michel Blanc, Gérard Lanvin, Sophie Duez. P. *83*.

Marraines de France, 1916. Prod.: Gaumont. Dir.: Léonce Perret. Starring: Fabienne Fabrèges, Yvette Andreyor. P. 29.

Mignon, vers 1906. Prod.: Gaumont. Dir.: Alice Guy. P. *17*.

Mille et Deuxième Nuit (La), 1933. Prod.: GFFA. Dir.: Alexandre Volkoff. Starring: Tania Fédor, Laure Savy, Ivan Mosjoukine, Gaston Modot. P. *45*.

Miracle des Loups (Le), 1924. Prod.: Société des Films Historiques. Dir.: Raymond Bernard. Starring: Yvonne Sergyl, Charles Dullin, Gaston Modot. P. *46*.

Mort au Champ d'Honneur, 1915. Prod.: Gaumont. Dir.: Léonce Perret. Starring: Fabienne Fabrèges, Paul Manson. P. 29.

My Father's Glory, 1990. Prod.: Gaumont, TF1 Films. Dir.: Yves Robert. Starring: Thérèse Liotard,

Philippe Caubère, Julien Ciamaca. P. *85*, 92.

My Mother's Castle, 1990. Prod.: Gaumont, Gaumont Prod., Prod. de la Gueville, TF1 Films prod. Dir.: Yves Robert. Starring: Thérèse Liotard, Julien Ciamaca, Philippe Caubère. P. 92.

Narayana, 1920. Prod.: Gaumont. Dir.: Léon Poirier. Starring: Edmond van Daële, Laurence Myrga. P.*30*.

Nikita, 1990. Prod.: Gaumont, Cecchi Gori Group. Dir.: Luc Besson. Starring: Jean-Hugues Anglade, Tcheky Karyo, Anne Parillaud, Jean Reno. P. 95.

Nostalghia, 1985. Prod.: RAI, Opera Film. Dir.: Andrzej Tarkovski. Starring: Domiziana Giordano. P. 81, *81*.

Nuit de Varennes (La), 1982. Prod.: Gaumont, Opera Films, FR3. Dir.: Ettore Scola. Starring: Jean-Louis Barrault, Harvey Keitel, Marcello Mastroianni, Hanna Shygulla. P. *87*.

Nuit des Espions (La), 1959. Prod.: SNEG, Zebra Film. Dir.: Robert Hossein. Starring: Robert Hossein, Marina Vlady. P. 69.

Ombre Déchirée (L'), 1921. Prod.: Gaumont. Dir.: Léon Poirier. Starring: Suzanne Despres, Roger Karl. P. *30*.

Onésime Débute au Théâtre, 1913. Prod.: Gaumont Dir.: Jean Durand. Starring: Ernest Bourbon, Berthe Dagmar. P. *22*, 25.

Opération Corned Beef (L'), 1991. Prod.: Gaumont, TF1 Films Production, Alter Films, Alpilles Production. Dir.: J.-Marie Poiré. Starring: Christian Clavier, Valérie Lemercier, Jean Reno. P. *95*.

Orpheline (L'), 1921. Prod.: Gaumont Dir.: Louis Feuillade. Starring: Georges Biscot, Greyjane, Fernand Hermann, Blanche Montel. P. *30*, 32.

Oscar, 1967. Prod.: Gaumont International Dir.: Edouard Molinaro. Starring: Louis de Funès, Agathe Natanson, Claude Rich. P. 74.

Page de Gloire (Une), 1915. Prod.: Gaumont Dir.: Léonce Perret. Starring: Fabienne Fabrèges, René Monti. P. *29*.

Pamir, le Toit du Monde (documentary), after 1929. Distr. Gaumont. P. *50*.

Parisette, 1922. Prod.: Gaumont. Dir.: Louis Feuillade. Starring: Georges Biscot, Edouard Mathé, Sandra Milowanoff. P. *32*.

Parsifal, 1982. Prod.: Gaumont, TMS Films. Dir.: Hans-Jurgens Syberberg. Starring: Edith Clever, Armin Jordan. P. 80.

Pendaison à Jefferson City, 1911. Prod.: Gaumont. Dir.: Jean Durand. Starring: Berthe Dagmar, Joe Hamman. P. *23*.

Pied qui Etreint (Le), 1916. Prod.: Gaumont. Dir.: Jacques Feyder. Starring: Kitty Hott, André Roanne. P. *32*.

Poilus de la Revanche (Les), 1916. Prod.: Gaumont. Dir.: Léonce Perret. Starring: Mario Nasthasio. P. 29.

Procès des Doges (Le), 1964. Prod.: SNEG, Ultra Films, Lux Films. Dir.: Duccio Tessari. Starring: Michèle Morgan, Jacques Perrin. P. 69.

Railway de la Mort (Le), 1912 . Prod.: Gaumont. Dir.: Jean Durand. Starring: Berthe Dagmar, Joe Hamman. P. *23.*

Rendez-vous de Juillet (Les), 1949. Prod.: SNEG, UGC. Dir.: Jacques Becker. Starring: Nicole Courcel, Daniel Gélin. P. *53*, 62.

Retour du Grand Blond (Le), 1974. Prod.: Gaumont. Dir.: Yves Robert. Starring: Mireille Darc, Pierre Richard, Jean Rochefort. P. *74*, 75.

Risques du Métier (Les), 1967. Prod.: Gaumont International Dir.: André Cayatte. Starring: Jacques Brel, Emmanuelle Riva. P. 74.

Romance à l'Inconnue, 1930. Prod.: GFFA. Dir.: René Barbéris. Starring: Annabella, Alain Guivel. P 45.

Roumanie, Terre d'Amour, 1930. Prod.: GFFA. Dir.: Camille de Morlhon. Starring: Raymond Destac, Pierre Nay, Renée Veller. P. *38*, 45.

Sahara (documentary), after 1929. Distr. GFFA. Dir.: Joseph Faivre. P. *50.*

Seul amour (Un), 1943. Prod.: SNEG. Dir.: Pierre Blanchar. Starring: Pierre Blanchar, Micheline Presle. P. 57.

Souricière (La), 1950. Prod.: SNEG, CCC. Dir.: Henri Calef. Starring: François Périer, Bernard Blier, Daniel Godet. P. 62.

Stalker, 1981. Prod.: Mosfilm-Sovexport. Distr. Gaumont. Dir.: Andrzej Tarkovski. Starring: Alexandre Kaidanovski, Anatoli Solonitsine. P. *81.*

Sur la Barricade, 1907. Prod.: Gaumont. Dir.: Alice Guy. P. 17.

Taxi pour Tobrouk (Un), 1961. Prod.: SNEG, Franco-London Film, Procusa, Continental Film. Dir.: Denys de la Patellière. Starring: Charles Aznavour, Hardy Krüger, Lino Ventura. P. 73.

Témoin dans la Ville (Un), 1959. Prod.: SNEG, Franco-London Film, Paris-Union Film, Tempo Film, Zebra Film. Dir.: Edouard Molinaro. Starring: Sandra Milo, Lino Ventura. P. 69.

Tendre et Violente Elisabeth, 1960. Prod.: Ceres-Films, Les Films Marly, SNEG. Dir.: Henri Decoin. Starring: Marie Déa, Paulette Dubost, Christian Marquand. P. 69.

Temptress (The), 1926. Prod.: Metro-Goldwyn. Distr.: GMG. Dir.: Fred Niblo. Starring: Lionel Barrymore, Greta Garbo. P. *34.*

Testament de Pierrot (Le), 1904. Prod.: Gaumont. Dir.: Alice Guy. P. *17.*

Tontons Flingueurs (Les), 1963. Prod.: SNEG, Corona Filmproduction, Ultra Films. Dir.: Georges Lautner. Starring: Bernard Blier, Francis Blanche, Sabine Sinjen, Lino Ventura. P. *67.*

Tragédie de la Mine (La), 1931. Prod.: GFFA, Nero-Film. Dir.: Georg-Willhem Pabst, Robert Beaudoin. Starring: Georges Charlia, Daniel Mendaille. P. *40.*

Traviata (La), 1983. Prod.: Accent Films. Dir.: Franco Zeffirelli. Starring: Teresa Stratas, Placido Domingo, Cornell Macneil. P. 81.

Triple Entente, 1915. Prod.: Gaumont. Dir.: Gaston Ravel. Starring: Musidora, Jean Signoret. P. 29.

Trois Font la Paire (Les), 1957. Prod.: Gaumont, CLM. Dir.: Sacha Guitry, Clément Duhour. Starring: Darry Cowl, Sophie Desmarets, Michel Simon. P. *65.*

Un, Deux Trois, Soleil, 1993. Prod.: Gaumont, Ciné Valse, France 3 Cinéma. Dir.: Bertrand Blier. Starring: Anouk Grinberg, Olivier Martinez, Marcel Mastroianni. P. *94.*

Union Sacrée (L'), 1915. Prod.: Gaumont. Dir.: Louis Feuillade. Starring: Lise Laurent, Edouard Mathé, Musidora. P. 29.

Vautrin, 1943. Prod.: SNEG. Dir.: Pierre Billon. Starring: Georges Marshal, Michel Simon, Madeleine Sologne. P. 57, *57.*

Vice et la Vertu (Le), 1963. Prod.: SNEG, Trianon Production. Dir.: Roger Vadim. Starring: Catherine Deneuve, Annie Girardot, Robert Hossein. P 69.

Vie de Paul Gauguin (La), 1978. Prod.: Téléproductions Gaumont. Dir.: Roger Pigault. Starring: Maurice Barrier, Anne Lonnberg. P. 89.

Visitors (The), 1993. Prod.: Gaumont, Alter Films, France 3 Cinéma, Alpilles Productions. Dir.: Jean-Marie Poiré. Starring: Christian Clavier, Valérie Lemercier, Jean Reno. P. 95, *95.*

Volée par les Bohémiens, 1905. Prod.: Gaumont. Dir.: Alice Guy. P. 17.

LOUIS DELLUC AWARDS

INDEX

PHOTOGRAPH CREDITS AND ACKNOWLEDGMENTS

All documents come from the Gaumont Museum and the Gaumont Cinémathèque, except the following images: Ciné Plus, Paris 48l. Christophe L., Paris 63br, 74al.
The author and Editions Gallimard are greatly indebted to Corine Faugeron and Marianne Chanel at the Gaumont Museum for their immense help, as well as Manuella Padoan at the Gaumont Cinémathèque. We would also like to thank Sarah Chayes for rereading all the book.
Editors: Cécile Dutheil de la Rochère, Nathalie Palma. Designers: Catherine Le Troquier; Dominique Guillaumin («Documents»).

Table of contents